ELEMENTS
OF
POLITICAL SCIENCE

Every good government's duty is to do more for the regions that are underdeveloped.

BY

BEN BOLFA

TABLE OF CONTENTS

CONTENTS PAGE

INTRODUCTION

Elements of Political Science

This edition is meant for undergraduate students in Political Science. This edition have been developed to meet global standards. This course guide gives you an overview of the course. It also provides you with relevant information on the organization and requirements of the course.

COURSE AIMS

The aims are to help you understand basic principles and concepts in Political Science. The broad aims will be achieved by:

(i) Introducing you to Political Science, its nature, scope and sub-divisions, as well as the validity or otherwise of the claim of Political Science to the status of a science.
Equip you with basic concepts in Political Science such as power, authority and legitimacy as well as sovereignty, including the important place they occupy in any political discourse, and how their use or mis-use can affect the workings of a political system

(ii) Examining the nature and character of the political systems of major developed countries, the manner they have contributed to relative political stability in these societies and how the knowledge gained from their experience can be applied to the politics of the developing world.

(iii) Exposing you to the knowledge of different forms of governments and ideologies and how they have contributed either to the expansion or denial of human rights or economic opportunities among different strata of the population

(iv) Enabling you to understand how peaceful and orderly political change can be brought about through widely acceptable procedure and agreed mechanism.

OBJECTIVES

To achieve the aims set out above, **ELEMENTS OF POLITICAL SCIENCE** has broad objectives. In addition, each unit also has specific objectives. The unit objectives are at the beginning of each unit. I advise that you read them before you start working through the unit. You may refer to them in the course of the unit to personally monitor your progress.

On successful completion of the course, you should be able to:

- define Political Science, its nature, scope and approaches, and how it developed through its systematic methodology into a Social Science discipline.
- understand the concepts of the state, nation and nation-state, their coercive and integrative roles in societies, as well as their differences and relationships.
- know the meanings of major concepts in Political Science, their usage and how they can be applied in political discourse.
- Understand the meanings and differences between power, authority and legitimacy
- appreciate the intrinsic merits of democracy as a preferable form of government that can facilitate the enthronement of a responsible government
- explain how political change can be brought about either through the conventional electoral process or through unorthodox revolutionary means.

WORKING THROUGH THIS COURSE

To complete the course you are required to read the study units and other related material. You will also need to undertake practical exercises for which you need a pen, a note-book, and other materials that will be listed in this guide. The exercises are to aid you, and to facilitate your understanding of the concepts and issues being presented. At the end of each unit, you will be required to submit written assignments for assessment purposes. At the end of the course, you will write a final examination.

COURSE MATERIALS

The major materials you will need for this course are:

- Course guide
- Study units
- Assignment file
- Relevant textbooks including the ones listed under each unit.

You may also need to listen to programme and news on the radio and television, local and foreign.

As a beginner, you need to read newspapers, magazines, journals and if possible log on to the internet.

HOW TO GET THE MOST FROM THIS TEXT

In distance learning, this edition replace the university lecture. This is one of the great advantages of distance learning; you can read and work through specially designed study materials at your own pace, and at a time and place that suits you best. Think of it as reading the lecture instead of listening to the lecturer. In the same way a lecturer might give you some reading to do, the study units tell you where to read, and which are your text materials or set books. You are provided exercises to do at appropriate points, just as a lecturer might give you an in-class exercise. Each of the study units follows a common format. The first item is an introduction to the subject matter of the unit, and how a particular unit is integrated with the other units and the course as a whole. Next to this is a set of learning objectives. These objectives let you know what you should be able to do by the time you have completed the unit. These learning objectives are meant to guide your study. The moment a unit is finished, you will significantly improve your chances of passing the course. The main body of the unit guides you through the required reading from other sources. This will usually be either from your set books or from a Reading section. The following is a practical strategy for working through the course. If you run into any trouble, telephone your tutor. Remember that your tutor's job is to help you. When you need assistance, do not hesitate to call and ask your tutor to provide it.

1.   Read this Course Guide thoroughly, it is your first assignment.
2.   Organize a Study Schedule. Design a 'Course Over' to guide you through the Course, Note the time you are expected to spend on each unit and how the Assignments relate to the units. Whatever method you choose, you should decide on and write in your own dates and schedule of work for each unit.
3.   Once you have created your own study schedule, do everything to stay faithful to it. The major reason why students fail is that they get behind with their course work. If you get into

difficulties with your schedule, please, let your tutor know before it is too late to help.

4   Turn to Unit I, and read the introduction and the objectives for the unit.

5.   Assemble the study materials. You will need your set books and the unit you are studying at any point in time. As you work through the unit, you will know what sources to consult for further information.

6.   Keep in touch with your study center. Up-to-date course information will be continuously available there.

7.   Well before the relevant due dates (about 4 weeks before due dates), keep in mind that you will learn a lot by doing the assignment carefully. They have been designed to help you meet the objectives of the course and, therefore, will help you pass the examination. Submit all assignments not later than the due date.

8.   Review the objectives for each study unit to confirm that you have achieved them, if you feel unsure about any of the objectives, review the study materials or consult your tutor.

9.   When you are confident that you have achieved a unit's objectives, you can start on the next unit. Proceed unit by unit through the course and try to pace your study so that you keep yourself on schedule.

10.   When you have submitted an assignment to your tutor's comments, both on the tutor-marked assignment form and also the written comments on the ordinary assignments.

11.   After completing the last unit, review the course and prepare yourself for the final examination. Check that you have achieved the unit objectives (listed at the beginning of each unit) and the course objectives (listed in the Course Guide

TUTORS AND TUTORIALS

Information relating to the tutorials will be provided at the appropriate time. Your tutor will mark and comment on your assignments, keep a close watch on your progress and on any difficulties you might encounter and provide assistance to you during the course. You must take your tutor-marked assignments to the study center well before the due date (at least two working days are required). They will be marked by your tutor and returned to you as soon as possible.

Do not hesitate to contact your tutor if you need help. Contact your tutor if you do not understand any part of the study units or the assigned readings

- You have difficulty with the exercises

- You have a question or problem with an assignment or with your tutor's comments on an assignment or with the grading of an assignment.

You should try your best to attend the tutorials. This is the only chance to have face-to-face contact with your tutor and ask questions which are answered instantly. You can raise any problem encountered in the course of your study. To gain the maximum benefit from course tutorials, prepare a question list before attending them. You will learn a lot from participating in discussion actively.

SUMMARY

The course guide gives you an overview of what to expect in the course of this study. The course teaches you the basic principles and concepts in Political Science. It also acquaints you with the central role of power as well as its limitations within the political process.

We wish you success with the course and hope that you will find it both interesting and useful.

**MAIN
TABLE OF
CONTENTS**

CONTENTS   PAGE

MODULE 1

UNIT   DEFINITION AND SCOPE OF POLITICAL SCIENCE

1.0   Introduction
2.0   Objectives
3.0   Main Contents
        3.1   Definitions of Political Science
        3.2   Basic Assumptions in Political Science
        3.3   Sub-divisions in Political Science
4.0   Summary
5.0   Conclusion
6.0   Tutor-Marked Assignments

1.0   INTRODUCTION

In this unit, we will attempt to offer different definitions of Political Science as an academic discipline. The unit also delineates the scope of Political Science to enable you understand and capture the essence and the major areas of concern to you as students of Political Science. The Unit also examines a set of assumptions that are germane and relevant to the understanding of the course. It further discusses the two sub-division of the discipline, which represents a modest attempt to relate the theory, or prescriptions (normative approach) with the practical (empirical approach) to the study of Political Science.

2.0   OBJECTIVES

At the end of this unit, you should be able to:

- define Political Science as an academic discipline
- categorize the discipline into its different components
- analyze the relationships between the different segments or divisions of the discipline, and how they overlap.

3.0   MAIN CONTENT

The whole essence of the first unit is to attempt to seriously examine and explain the component parts of Political Science. In other words, this unit is an attempt to identify what is studied in the discipline or its "content" and its "structure" or how the content is studied. The first thing to know is the concept of "politics" or the "political", while the second the suffix, "science", which will form the subject matter of the next unit. When Political Scientists examine the meanings attached to these concepts, they in effect seek to conceptualize, or understand the discipline and also delineate the boundaries of Political Science.

In the course of the development of the discipline, a number of political philosophers and political scientists has advanced a number of definitions. Most of the definitions can be classified as being of two types. Some scholars associate "politics" with "government", "legal government", or the "state", while others discuss it within the precinct of "power", "authority" and/or "conflict". We shall consider a few of these definitions, offer a critique of them, or their limitations, and leave you to determine which of them have more contemporary relevance to the understanding of Political Science.

3.1   Different definitions of Political Science

A good starting point is to ask the question: what is politics? Every citizen appears to have a commonsense notion of what politics is. However, some Political Scientists are unsatisfied with the common sense meaning of politics as they believe that in order to really gain knowledge of politics one should formulate a more explicit definition of politics as failure to do so, in their view, restrict the growth of Political Science. Their position is that Political Science should be contextually examined. This suggests that the outer limits of Political Science can be determined by listing all the topics, which interest scholars in the field at a given time.

One view is Politics as Government: To an average citizen, politics and government are synonymous. In Alfred de Grazia's view "politics" or the "political" includes the events that happened around the decision – making centres of government. Charles Hyneman also said that most Political Scientists have assumed that legal government is the subject matter of their discipline. However, if Political Scientists equate "politics" with "government" or "legal government", we need to know what we mean by government. Government in this context refers to the legally based institutions of a society, which may make legally binding decisions. This merely shows that Hyneman's definition is more specific than that of de Grazia. Whichever definition a Political Scientist may eventually decide to adopt, what is obvious is that this definition focuses more on formal institutions than any other thing else.

We must however caution that a definition that equates politics with government has a commonsensical basis, which has serious limitations. This is because it is inadequate and restrictive in scope. For instance, if a Political Scientist elects to study the politics of the pre-colonial African society, he would be examining ethnic societies with no governmental institutions. Yet, the traditional rulers and elders within such societies would be seen to be making political decisions for the community but not within identifiable and elaborate political and legal institutions, such as parliament, congress and courts. Since such actions are taken out of government or state, are they to be classified as non-political? This obviously makes the definition narrow and hence dangerous for you. In an attempt to escape this weakness, there is a need to look beyond governmental institutions for the elements that make or qualify an activity as political. This takes us to David Easton's definition, which emphasizes the kind of activity that expresses itself through a variety of institutions.

David Easton's view of politics

The crux of the definition advocated by the Eastonian school is the equation of politics with "power," "authority" or "conflict." Foremost in this school is William Bluhm, a Political Scientist, who defined politics "as a social process characterized by activity involving rivalry and co-operation in the exercise of power, culminating in the making of decision for a group." The appeal of this definition is its apparent flexibility or wider scope. It sees politics wherever power relationships or conflicts situation exist. This means that the Political Scientists can legitimately study the politics of a labour or students union, corporations or Africa tribe/or ethnic group as well as what goes on in the legislature arm, or administrative agency. Here, emphasis is placed on activity or behaviour rather than a particular kind of institution.

A step further from the restrictive "government" definition and the "power" variety takes us to David Easton's definition, which sees politics as the "authoritative allocation of values for a society" within the political system. This definition restricts the Political Scientist to only those decisions, which are authoritative for the society. According to Easton, "a policy is authoritative if when the person to whom it is intended to apply, or who are affected by it considers that they must or ought to obey it" ( ). In other words, such a policy must be considered binding. However, not every authoritative decision is made within the political system. Following from Easton's definition, it means that the

Political Scientist is only interested in the authoritative decisions which apply to all members of the society, although only a few might be affected (Dahl 1984).

Harold Laswell view of politics

Politics, in one of its lucid definitions by Harold Lasswell (1936) is 'the study of who gets what, when, and how"? The unfolding picture is that there is no major difference between Easton's definition and the one based on power. Both of them assume a political world of scarce values and insatiable appetites. The basic question of politics then becomes: "How are values distributed?" or in Harold Laswell's classic phraseology, "who gets what, when, and how?" The difference is mainly one of emphasis. Whereas, the power theorists such as Lasswell emphasise the role of power in the distribution process, the Eastonian variant or typology examines the relationship between what goes into a system "demand" and what comes out as "decision", or "output". Thus, Easton while focuses his attention on the entire political system; Laswell on the other hand concentrates on individuals who have the greatest impact in the distribution process, namely those with power. The over-riding argument for an Eastonian type definition of politics is based on the desirability of a compromise position, which is not too restrictive or overly broad. This does not mean that the Estonian definition is free from criticism. Its critics have asked what is meant by decision "for society", and how this differs from one which is not made for society. To many Political Scientists, any elaborate attempt to answer these questions is a mere academic exercise or even superfluous.

Aristotle's view of Politics

Politics arises, according to Aristotle, in organized states, which recognize themselves to be an aggregate of many members, not a single tribe, religion, interest, or tradition. Politics arises from accepting the fact of the simultaneous existence of different traditions, within a territorial unit under a common rule. According to Aristotle, politics is a plausible response to the problem of governing, or maintaining order, in a complex society. However, the establishing of order is not just any order at all; politics if properly played marks the end of tyranny and recognition of freedom. To him politics represents as least some tolerance of opposing views and, indeed best conducted, where open canvassing of rival interests is allowed and possible.

Politics, as Aristotle pointed out, is only one possible solution to the problem of order. Tyranny - the rule of one strong man in his own interest, oligarchy - the rule of one group in their own interest are alternatives, which he did not approve of. The method of rule of a tyrant and oligarchy is to coerce all or most of these other groups for their own personal benefit. The political method of rule is to listen to these other groups to conciliate, or reconcile them as far as possible, and to give them a legal position, a sense of security, some clear and reasonable safe means of articulation. More importantly, Aristotle view politics as the "master science." Politics is the master science not in the sense that it includes or explains all other sciences, but in that, it gives them some priority. The way of establishing these priorities is by allowing the right institutions to develop by which the various "science" can demonstrate their actual importance in the common task of survival.

SELF-ASSESSMENT EXERCISE 1

Define Political Science and examine the most significant theme of Aristotle's opinion of Political Science.

3.2   Basic Assumptions in Political Science

There are some assumptions, if properly noted that will help you in the understanding of political science both as an academic discipline and as a practical endeavor. The first assumption is that all human societies are faced with the problem of scarce resources. Whether the primary resource is wealth, status or power, demand always exceeds supply. The second assumption is that in order to prevent conflict resulting from distribution of scarce resources from destroying the fabric of society, the dominant groups in all societies evolves a mechanism, generally referred to as governments to sort this out. This mechanism, otherwise known as government may range from the massive governments apparatus of modern industrialized states such as United States, Britain, or Japan, or through the simple headship of a simple, undifferentiated ethnic group in Africa.

The third assumption is that government allocates resources to some individuals while depriving others. Accordingly, policies pursued by governments are inherently unequal. This is true in both authoritarian and democratic states. It is equally true of socialist and capitalist societies. The fourth assumption is that constant pressure exists for the re-allocation of scarce resources. Whether it takes the form of civil war, riot, voting, or diffused grumbling, pressure by the 'have-not' for the reallocation of resource is pervasive in all societies. The fifth assumption is that because of the pervasive pressure by the 'have-not' for the allocations of resources, those individuals who benefit from the existing distribution of resources in the society, the 'haves', actively engage in pervasive efforts to maintain the *status quo* while the "have-nots" seek to overthrow the system.

The sixth assumption is that the more the rulers of a society can persuade the masses that the established system of government is legitimate, just and really serves the best interest of the masses, the more secured the position of the ruler otherwise and the halves will be in a pervasive struggle with the 'have-nots The rulers of all societies thus attempt to secure their privileged positions by justifying their right to rule in terms of a grand religious or national myth, usually developed as a rallying point.

Taken collectively, the above assumptions stress the dynamics nature of the political process. Politics is therefore the constant interplay between the rulers (elite) and the ruled (masses). Politics is also pervasive conflict among competing institutions such as parliaments, political parties; courts etc that are the institutionalized focal points of this struggle. For the elite, formal institution, are the means of controlling the masses and of securing their position against the competing elites. For the masses, formal institutions symbolize the status quo and are primary target of change. Also because formal political institutions are the focal point of political conflict, they too are in a constant pressure to adapt to change, and such changes may be peaceful, as in the evolution of American and Britain political institutions, or abrupt and violent, as in the case of many third world countries in Africa, Asia and Latin America, and may even include the implosion of the political institutions and structures as was witnessed in the former Soviet Union in 1991.

Underlining the assumptions above is the unstated but vital role of human activity, or what is technically called political behaviour in the completely political process. The conflict over scarce resources that lies at the heart of the political process is a conflict between or among human beings. It is human beings (as elites) who utilize control and manipulate the formal political institutions of society and it is human beings (as masses) who are both the object of elite control and the pervasive threat to its existence. The removal of the human element from the political equation would render any political analysis a sterile exercise or endeavor.

SELF-ASSESSMENT EXERCISE 2

Explain how Political Science is related to Economics

3.3   Sub-divisions of Political Science

Political Science can be broadly grouped into two divisions: political theory and political organization. The concern of political theory, otherwise known as the normative aspect is to provide answers to question like: what are the purposes of political organizations? What are the best means of realizing them? What is the nature of the authority of the state? Has the state unlimited power? How do we reconcile the authority of the state with the liberty of the citizens? The answers to these different posers constitute the pre-occupation of political philosophers such as Plato, Aristotle, Thomas Hobbes, J. J Rousseau etc. In short, these scholars were concerned with the formulation of the ends and limits of authority (Appadiorai, 1981:3-12).

The second division of Political Science- political organization - otherwise known as empirical studies focuses on the organization of government. Government is the instrument by which the purpose of the state is realized. The form and workings of government differ from one country to the other. Over the years, forms of government have ranged from monarchy, aristocracy, through oligarchy to democracy. A country like Britain for example practices constitutional monarchy and yet, to all intents and purposes, qualifies to be described as democratic government. The United States, on the other hand, operates a republican democracy having no room for a king. Before the break-up of the Soviet Union, her form of government was essentially an oligarchy of a select few, who constituted the top hierarchy of the Communist party (Almond et al, 2005: 40-43).

In all forms of government what is common to them is power: how power is acquired, retained, consolidated or lost. While the retention of power is the preoccupation of the rulers, what is of more relevance to the ruled is the use or abuse/misuse of power. History tells us, and as confirmed by Lord Action, that 'power corrupts and absolute power corrupts absolutely'. Therefore, to guard against abuse of power, most societies provide institutional and constitutional safeguards, to check the possible excesses of government. In America, for example, the constitution enshrined the systems of separation of powers and checks and balances while the British unwritten constitution recognizes conventions including parliamentary enactments, meant to secure the liberty of the citizens. Without these forms of restraints on the authority of government as well as the rights of the citizens, the society will degenerate either into rule of men, rather than law, or into the other extreme of anarchy, which Thomas Hobbes described as a "state of nature."

SELF-ASSESSMENT EXERCISE 3

Differentiate between the normative and empirical studies of Political Science.

4.0   SUMMARY

In this unit, we gave some definitions of Political Science as an academic discipline. We also discussed some basic assumptions that are made in the study of the course, and without which Political science will be devoid of the rigor that is expected of an academic discipline. The Unit also outlined the two broad divisions of Political Science that has made it a nice blend of the theory and practice of politics.

5.0   CONCLUSION

Like every other course in the Social Sciences or Humanities, it is not possible to have a generally acceptable definition of Political Science. Indeed, every definition no matter how it outwardly claims to approximate the reality of the discipline remains a mere attempt at a formulation. Therefore, in order to do justice to the requirements of this course you need to blend some of these definitions, bearing in mind their respective shortcomings, and hoping that this remains the only way to get at near holistic understanding of the discipline.

6.0   TUTOR-MARKED ASSIGNMENTS

1.   Explain the relevance of Harold Lasswell's definition in the understanding of Political Science.
2.   Discuss political science in the normative and positive perspectives.
3.   Critically analyze the symbiotic relationship between politics and economics.

UNIT 2   NATURE AND STATUS OF POLITICAL SCIENCE

1.0   INTRODUCTION

In spite of many decades of the study of political science, especially the development of the behavioral approach to the discipline, the debate has not subsided on the correct status of the discipline. Notwithstanding its well-developed scientific methodology, there are those who still hold to the view that it is premature to describe political science as a science discipline since several aspects of its teachings, especially its practice, qualifies it as an art. This unit, in its different sections, without attempting to finally resolve the age-long controversy, only seeks to explore further the debate in order to state what appears to be the most plausible or popular view among scholars.

2.0   OBJECTIVES

- at the end of this unit, you should be able to:
- analyze meaningfully whether politics is a pure or social science discipline
- explain reasonably on its appropriate status as a social science discipline
- discuss the relationships between political science and other disciplines and how its study and teachings have benefitted from them.

3.0   MAIN CONTENT

3.1   The subject matter of science

First, we need to know the subject matter of science, or to put it differently what is science? Science is a branch of knowledge or study dealing with a body of facts or truths systematically arranged and showing the operation of general laws. Science therefore collects or gathers facts and links them together in their causal sequence with the objective of drawing valid inferences. A scientific knowledge is therefore based on reason and evidence, as well as conclusions that are verifiable, communicable and can be replicated across national frontiers. Any scientific discipline must therefore possess the following characteristics:

- The possibility of a consistent, concise and connected formulation.
- The capacity to generalize and make predictions.
- The possibility of verification of the data as well as the generalizations.
- An agreement on methods, and
- The adequate training of those who are engaged in scientific work.

Comparative Politics, one of the major branches of Political Science is a field of study where the five listed above characteristics of a science discipline best apply; the other three branches are Political Theory, Public administration and International Relations. For example, in Comparative Politics there is what is called some minimal scientific requirements for any comparative analysis. They include definition of terms and accurate description of the subject matter of study, formulation of hypothesis in form of a causal relationship (if A, then B), acceptance, rejection or modification of hypothesis when tested with available data. When an hypothesis is accepted a grand theory of politics may be developed that can be used for either a single country or cross-country study.

The scientific approach in Political Science therefore refers to the methods being employed by the practitioners of the discipline. It should be noted that the methodology which a Political Scientist adopts, and the basic assumptions he makes will, to some extent, influence the image he has of his discipline. This is because "scope" and "method" cannot be completely divorced - they are intertwined. Methodology can and should be studied in its own right but in addition, it ought to be considered as an important influence on the scope of Political Science, especially as methodology indicates, not what the discipline is but, to some extent, what Political Science can and cannot do.

SELF-ASSESSMENT EXERCISE 1

Explain the major criteria or requirements of a scientific discipline.

3.2   The status of Political Science

Political science is a social science discipline because it deals with human beings. It is different from the natural or physical sciences, which deal with matters, atoms and molecules. Unlike the natural sciences like physics, chemistry and biology where the laws governing them are uniform, exact and certain; this is not so in the social sciences like Politics, Economics, Geography and Sociology whose central theme is human beings. For these reasons the premises or assumptions of Political Science are weak, its conclusions at best, tentative, and at worst, dubious. In spite of these limitations what qualifies Political Science as a Social Science discipline is its reliance on scientific methods of research. By describing political concepts, testing and using of hypothesis to make forecast or predict future phenomenon, which can be generalized across nations, subject to some environmental variables. Political Science relies on knowledge gained from other disciplines like Economics, Sociology, Geography, History etc. to build hypothesis and formulate theories. History, for example is usually regarded as the laboratory of Political Science. As professor Seeley aptly puts it, "Political Science is the fruit of history and History is the root of Political Science. A number of assumptions and principles characterize Sciences or scientific methods. First, scientists assume some laws or principles of determinism or law of universal causation. This means that Political Scientist who accepts scientific methods plunges into his work assuming that nothing in politics just happens. The second major characteristic of science is its empirical basis. This implies a number of features, including an observational foundation, inter-subjectivity, and the value free nature of science. The objectives of science are summarized in its characteristics of being systematic in nature, its empirical generalizations, development of systematic theory and finally explanations and predictions.

However, the arguments against the possibility of a science of politics invariably attempts to demonstrate that Political Science does not/or cannot have one or more of these characteristics. The controversy generated by this latter view (which we shall return to and examine in detail in the next section) is that political science by its nature does not possess the character of a science discipline. Those who hold this position have gone to the extent of advising behaviorally oriented political scientists to abandon all pretences, put the brakes on their fantasies, admit the futility of their efforts, and return to the traditional ways of doing things. The table below draws comparisms and contrasts between the Social and Natural Sciences.

S/N	Social Sciences	Natural Sciences
1.	Economics, Politics, Sociology, etc.	Physics,Chemistry,Biology, Mathematics, etc.,
2.	Studies Man as Social Beings in a given	Studies nature through Matter, Atoms and Molecules
3.	Uses scientific methods as tools of analysis	Uses scientific methods as tools of analysis
4.	No certainty or universal validity of results or	There is universal validity of results and prediction
5.	No precise definition of concepts, it is subject to some endogenous variables,	Concepts are uniform and standard irrespective of the environments, e.g. Law of Gravity, Pythagoras Theorem and Formulae
6.	Uses the field as laboratory without special tools or instruments for the	Laboratories are in a controlled room with specialized tools and chemicals
7.	No agreement on methodology of research	There is agreement on methodology of research and level of training
8.	Research work are affected by sentiments, habits, moods	Research work are not affected by sociological, political or any sentiment

SELF-ASSESSMENT EXERCISE 2

Discuss those features, which qualify Political Science as an academic discipline.

3.3 The Science or Art debate or controversy on the status of Political Science

From what we have discussed above, it is obvious that any scientific discipline is concerned with rational and systematic organization of ideas. You need to understand that to the extent that politics remains the study of human activities and interactions as it relates to the struggle to seek and retain power through legitimate means, we can say it qualifies to be described as a science discipline. In addition, as far as the political behaviour of some practitioners

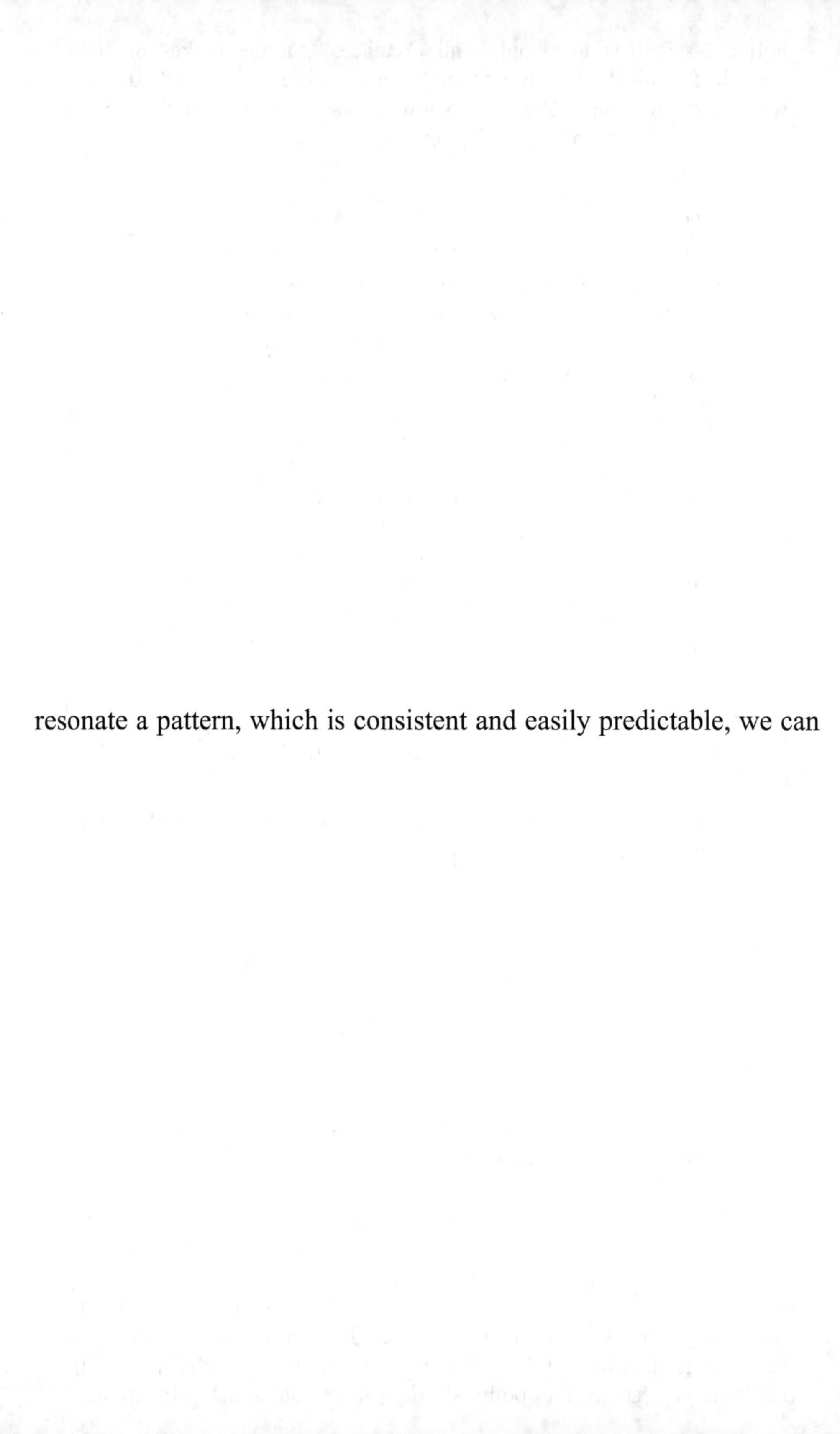

resonate a pattern, which is consistent and easily predictable, we can also say that the tenets or requirements of science have been met. From the array of studies that are carried out by Political Scientists, it is possible to discern a pattern, or develop a theory from which assumptions, deductions or inferences as well as generalizations and conclusions can be drawn. We can also develop models or ideal-constructs, which can be verified or replicated in other societies with little or no modifications. To this extent, we are right to conceive politics as a science discipline.

The interdisciplinary approach also states that there is an inescapable, yet beneficial relationships among the major social science disciplines, be it Economics, Psychology, Sociology or Anthropology. This will be taken on more rigorously in the next section. In spite of this symmetry or linkage among the various disciplines, however, the central issues in the study of Political Science can still be identified. They include power, how it is acquired and used; authority and legitimacy, how it is secured and maintained. Nation-state and supra-national organizations, how they can be made to survive and, Governmental institutions, how they are structured, organized and interrelated.

But, before we jump into the conclusion about the status of political science as a scientific discipline, we must recognize the complexity of political phenomena and what is called "human indeterminacy". First, a major point that has been raised against the science of politics is that it is difficult to discover regularities about political phenomena and this is in addition to a variety of meanings or usages usually ascribed to political concepts, which often makes their meaning unclear or less precise. Second, Russel Kirk is a foremost critic of the science of politics, when he argued: "Human beings are the least controllable, verifiable, law obeying and predictable of subjects". Kirk's argument strikes at the presence of freedom in politics, which makes it possible for individuals to be free to choose their course of action at any given point in the political process. For this reason, it will therefore be difficult for such behaviour to be classified making generations and formulations of theories on such behavior difficult.

In spite of the above, we can still make a proposition on this art or science controversy thus: if the study of Political Science is systematic, the practice of politics appears to have the characteristics of an art in the developed climes, and close to an organized chaos in the developing world. Most rulers in Africa for example, often conceive politics from the perspective of Isaac Disrael who defines politics as the "art of governing mankind by deceiving them" (Crick, 1962:16) or Harold Lasswell who took a trip from his popular and apt definition of politics, and described a politician as "a person with private motives, translated into public objects and rationalized as being in the public interest".

Politics thus becomes the rationalization human interests, as embodied in institutional relationships, which are presented to be for the promotion of public good. Indeed, what politics and leadership has been turned into in developing societies are clearly very different from the Aristotle's view of politics as an ennobling and elevating human activity, or that of Jeremy Bentham who conceived politics as "a means of achieving the greatest good for the greatest number."

Even in the advanced democracies, political dishonesty especially during elections, has reached such a height of sophistication that it is possible for political leadership to deceive their people. The manipulation is done by appealing to different primordial sentiments to persuade the populace to become uncritical supporters of the government of the day, no matter how narrow, self-centered or ruinous its policies might be. However, when the trend of deceit becomes persistent, citizens begin to view the government with disdain and may even encourage them to resort to disloyalty. It would be interesting to know why citizens may resort to anarchism. Government is created to strive for the wellbeing of the people in the polity apart from maintaining peace and orderliness in the society. However, when government becomes an impediment to the fulfillment of human potentials, the alternative is to either eliminate the government in parts or abolish it completely. It is also important to note that the institutions and apparatus of the state as well as their operators do not operate in a value free setting, and if they are not properly structured to reflect the common will they may be hijacked by a cabal for selfish ends rather than the interest of the generality of the people. There must be goals, which every society must set for itself that include order, justice and progress. We may want to know who sets the goals for a society and what criteria are used to determine the set goals? It is here that subjectivism, which violates the objective approach of a normal scientific inquiry is introduced. In practical terms, what is accorded primacy will depend on the level already attained by the people of a given society, although no country can endure for too long if any of these goals is consistently sacrificed for another. Therefore, only a carefully scientifically moderated and less mechanical approach to political science can make the discipline become relevant to the specific needs of every society.

It is possible that the undiscerning and less elevated scholar or student will consider the issue of ethics to be outside the purview of political science or even outside the realms of science generally. This is not true in reality. For instance, in spite of the Machiavellian popular phrase that "the end justifies the means", there is also the equally plausible proposition that "what is morally wrong cannot be politically right". Indeed, we cannot separate ethics from politics because the foundation of effective human authority over fellow human beings has both moral and ethical content. Where morality is impaired, authority is ineffective. In any case, the goal of justice cannot be attained if the leadership is not attuned to the acceptable moral and ethical norms of the society. We will explore this further when we discuss the relationships between Political Science and other disciplines in the section that follows.

SELF-ASSESSMENT EXERCISE 3

Critically examine whether Political Science is an art or social science discipline.

3.4   Political Science and other disciplines

3.4.1 Political Science and History

E. H. Carr defined history as "the unending dialogue between the present and the past." Professor Renier laid stress on the social role of history and so defined the discipline as "the memories of societies" (Rao, 2004:1-2). While making comparism between the two disciplines Professor Seely J. R. stated that Political Science is the fruit of history and history is the root of Political Science. For this reason, Political Scientists rely on historical facts to make predictions, and to carry out the whole gamut of the challenges posed in comparative political analysis. Professor R. G. Collingwood conceives the explorative role of history thus: "Science is finding things out: and in that sense history is science". In this vein since political Science also seeks to find things out, we can say the two disciplines do make relentless search for truth.

In his own comparism of Political Science and History, Sidgwick wrote: "The primary interest of history is the presentation of facts; the primary interest of politics is abstract, the formulation of general law and principle." Harold Laski once remarked in his treatise on human rights that "it is a lesson of history that people who are denied a share in political power are also denied a share in the benefit of power." Therefore, history constitutes a consistent and fertile source of political analysis and predictions.

3.4.2 Political Science and Ethics

Ethics is a branch of study that investigates the laws of morality and formulates the rule of conduct, that is what is right and wrong, the dos and don'ts. The utilitarian doctrine of Jeremy Bentham who prescribes "the greatest happiness of the greatest numbers" as the purpose of government better illustrates the union of ethics and politics. Moreover, when Harold Laski stated that rebellion is a contingent obligation of citizenship, he was only recommending this extreme option to a government that violates the social contract. Indeed, from Socrates to St. Thomas Aquino, the defining characteristic of political thinking was the presumed unity of ethics and politics. However, the general thrust of modern political thought from Machiavelli until date has been to call into question that presumption.

While Socrates said, there is such a thing as moral excellence that will produce, not simply limited happiness, but complete happiness, Aristotle believed that the state ought to possess an ethical character. Indeed, Aristotle believed that while the state comes into existence for the sake of life, it continues to exist for the sake of good life. Ideology, which is a political weapon, therefore seeks to reaffirm the unity of ethics and politics. On the other hand, in advising that the Prince should eschew ethical standards, Machiavelli believes in the actions of men, and especially princes, from where there is no appeal, the end justifies the means. It was in a reaction to Machiavelli's a-moral and desperate bid to deny humanity's essential ethical capacity that led to the development of ideologies. A former United States Secretary of State, James Baker (1995) shared this view of the unity of politics and ethics when he stated, "it is only through politics that we can transform philosophy into policy."

3.4.3 Political Science and Economics

Briefly defined, Economics is the science of wealth; it is concerned with the allocation and use of limited resources among the various groups in a society. Thus, while money is the currency of economics, power is the currency of politics and both are scarce in relation to the desire for them. The acquisition of both necessarily engenders competition, and setting of the rules to prevent conflict in order to achieve economic prosperity or political stability. Economics and politics intersect at many points because the political leadership takes vital economic decisions in a country, even in a capitalist system. The enduring lesson of the Great Depression of the 1930s and the global economic meltdown of 2007/8 is that it is dangerous for any government to allow a free reign of market forces, there is the need for some forms of regulation or intervention by the state to maintain the equilibrium. Not a few hold the view that American economic prosperity can only be better explained on the account of her stable political system. It is also believed that the more well-to-do a nation is, the greater her chances of political stability, all things being equal. In the immediate post-independence era in Ghana, Kwame Nkrumah was of the opinion that political freedom did not automatically deliver better life to his people, he qualified his often-quoted statement: "seek you first the political kingdom and every other thing shall be added unto it" with "political independence is meaningless without economic self-determination." Using democracy as a variable, Nkrumah further explained the link between politics and economics thus: "economic growth is a condition for the growth of democracy, not for its establishment." It is therefore safe to conclude that Politics and Economics are like Siemens twins in that there could hardly be political stability without economic prosperity and the economy can hardly grow without political stability, both must co-operate in order to produce a good result.

3.4.4 Political Science and Law

Political Science as a discipline can also be meaningful within the context of law, or what is known as constitutional order. It is well known that no society can be governed without the constitution either written or unwritten being the legal basis of authority in a society. The legislative processes in the parliament, the enforcement or implementation of law by the executive, as well as the business of interpretation of the constitution by the judiciary are major areas where political science and law intersects.

3.4.5 Political Science and Geography

Since Alfred Thayer and Sir Halford Mackinder coined the term geo-politics to explain the interaction of politics and human geography, the relationships between the two disciplines has not been in doubt, and has become widely accepted. Both scholars have particularly stressed the deterministic relationship between a country's geographical endowments and its foreign policy reflexes. It is a fact today that the wealth and power of a nation is a function, among other factors, of its location. Resources are located within the territorial confines of a state, and territory is an attribute of a state within which its citizens live, over which its government rules and exercises sovereignty.

3.4.6 Political Science and Sociology

Just as political science borrowed concepts such as centripetal and centrifugal forces from physics, or system analysis from biology, it has taken from sociology a popular conceptual framework known as structural functionalism that is particularly relevant in comparative political analysis. Indeed, the idea of socialization of societal norms and values, a major area of study in sociology is of relevance to political science, without which no society will achieve congruence or balance. Political Scientists have also adopted Max Weber's typologies of authority in their common endeavor with sociologists to distinguish between power and authority, the former being a central concept in political science.

SELF-ASSESSMENT EXERCISE 4

Distinguish between political science and other social sciences.

4.0   SUMMARY

In this unit, we have discussed the nature of political science and established that s is as a social science discipline. We have taken this position notwithstanding, or without prejudice to the debate on whether political science is an art or a science discipline. In line with the interdisciplinary approach often adopted in Social Science faculty, we also examined the relationships between political science and other disciplines, an engagement that has helped to deepen the breadth and rigor of political discourse and analysis.

5.0   CONCLUSION

The debate on whether political science is an art or science discipline may not be resolved quickly; the reason being that the borderlines between disciplines, even those in the natural sciences are fast collapsing. What has become clear today is that the whole universe or body of knowledge has its origin from one source, and they became fragmented into different disciplines as the world is evolving in complexity. The need to grapple with specific human problems and challenges has therefore made areas of specialization and narrowing down of fields imperative.

6.0   TUTOR-MARKED ASSIGNMENTS

1. Discuss how political science benefits from other academic disciplines.
2. Explain the accuracy or otherwise of Aristotle's description of Political Science as "Master Science"
3. Enumerate your reasons why we should surrender to the claims that political science is not a science discipline.

UNIT 3 EVOLUTION AND METHODS OF POLITICAL SCIENCE

1.0 INTRODUCTION

Political Science did not start as a full-fledged discipline. Like every other field of study, it began as an adjunct or a branch of a matured, older discipline. But after a deserving period of infancy and tutelage, it was nurtured and developed into maturity, having acquired enrichment both in content and methodology. This Unit examines the history, evolution and methods of political science, with particular reference to the different approaches that have dominated the different phases in the evolution, development and maturity of the discipline.

2.0 OBJECTIVES

At the end of this unit, you should be able to:

- explain the history and evolution of political science as a discipline from infancy to adulthood
- discuss the different approaches you can adopt to study the disciplines
- analyze other various methods to carry out academic enquiries into different aspects of political science.

3.0 MAIN CONTENT

3.1 Evolution of Political Science

3.1.1 The Era of Traditionalism in Political Science

Political science is a branch of social science. It developed from a mere descriptive and prescriptive area of knowledge to a scientific status, with

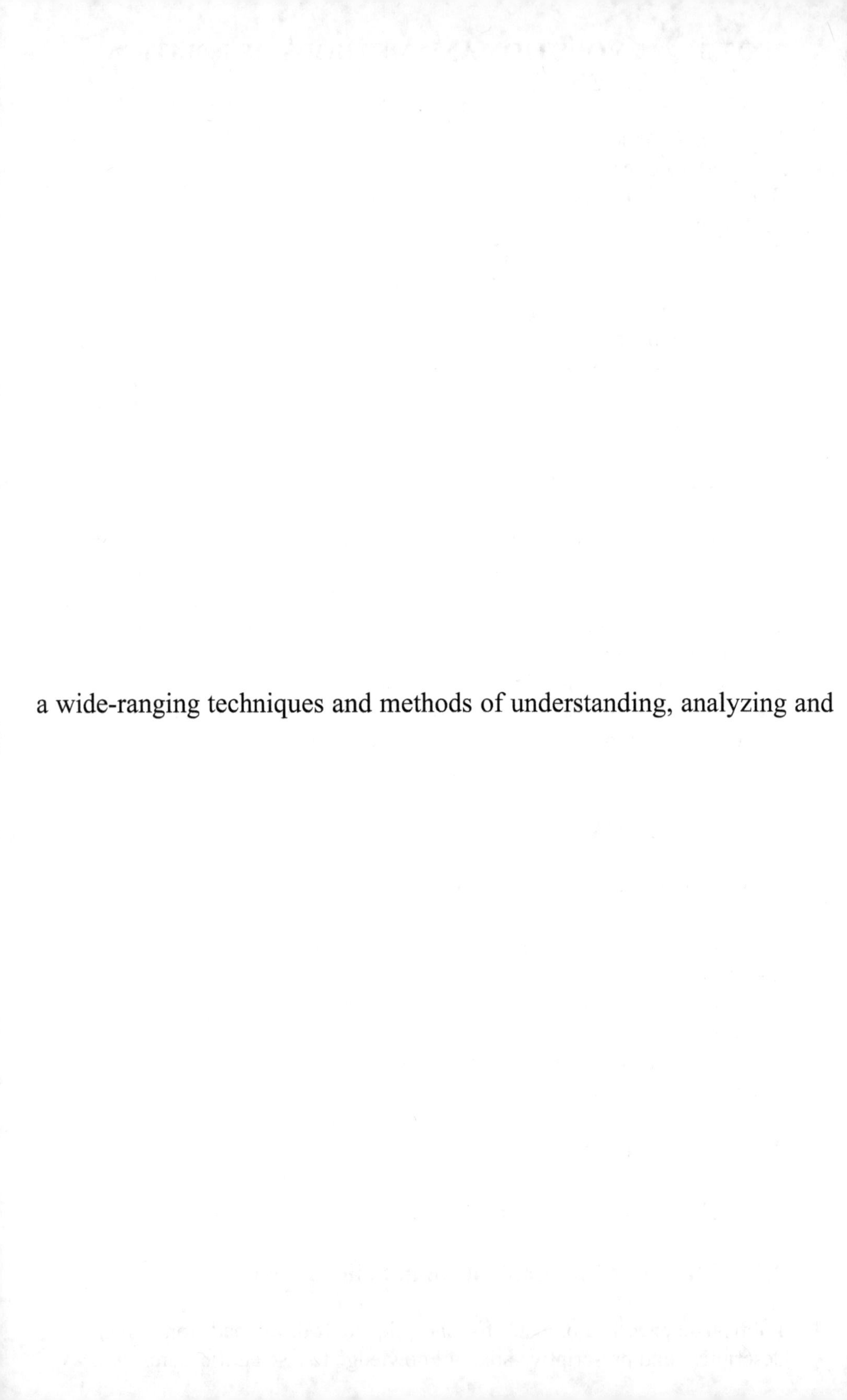

a wide-ranging techniques and methods of understanding, analyzing and predicting political phenomenon. Rodee, et al in their book, *Introductionto Political Science* noted that the term political science could be traced to Jean Bodin (1530-1596), a French political philosopher and lawyer who termed the study of politics "Science Politique" and gave Political science an abiding concern for the organization of institutions related to law. Another French, Philosopher, Montesquieu (1689 - 1755) argued that all functions of government could be encompassed within the categories of legislation, execution and the adjudication of law.

The term Political Science is one of the oldest in the pedigree of social sciences in particular, and sciences in general (Varma, 1975: 1, Dryzek and Leonard, 1988: 1246). In a more deductive sense, we can say that political science as an academic field of study, originated from the works of the ancient Greek philosophers whose major preoccupation was how to create an ideal state (Varma 1975: 1), or to avoid what was later described by social contract theorists as the state of nature. However, this is not to suggest that the study of politics in the ancient Greek city- states was the study of the "Science" of politics, as it is known in modern times. Rather, the main preoccupation of political thinkers of the time was historical and descriptive understanding of political phenomena.

Thus, in order to understand the different phases in the development of the field of political science Varma (1975:1) has clearly delineated four characteristic features of classical tradition to the understanding of political science - the historical - analytical, legal-institutional, normative -prescriptive, and descriptive taxonomy. Mbah (2007:28-9) also identified five main phases in the development and evolution of the discipline: the philosophical and deductive phase, the historical and comparative phase, juridical and constitutional phase, the observational and measurement phase and the psychological phase. Political science has therefore developed from historical perspective of dealing with the study of past and present political phenomena, and with a view to predicting the future of political processes. The first political scientist known to have analyzed information systematically was the Greek philosopher, Aristotle. He compared the constitutions of Greek city-states during the 4th century B.C. and generalized about the political consequences of the different constitutional systems (Appadorai, 2004).

The study of Political Science also flourished in ancient Greece during the 5th and 4th centuries B.C. in the Roman republic from 509 to 31B.C. in the republic of Italy during the 15th and 16th centuries, amidst the political turmoil of 17th century Britain, and during the French and American Revolutions towards the end of the 18th century. The concern of political scientists then was how to provide useful advice to rulers on how to organize government more effectively.

However, Political Science as it is studied and taught today was developed more recently. In the 19th century, Germany, academics developed a systematic science called "Staatlehre" to provide useful information to governments. The first Professor of Political Science in the United States was German emigre Francie Lieber, who was appointed Chairman of Political Science at Columbia College (now Columbia University) in New York City, in 1857.

The next generation of Political Scientists sought to establish the discipline's identity and influence in the emerging American university system, rather than through the America government. During 1920s and 1930s, Charles E. Merriam and his colleagues at the University of Chicago in Chicago formed the Chicago School. Merriam's many interests included the history of political thought and education. Most notably Harold Gosnell and Harold Lasswell conducted researches that focused on voting, mass political participation, the psychology of political behavior, leadership and wartime propaganda.

3.1.2 The Era of Behavioral Revolution

The Chicago school was the forerunner of what became known as the behavioral revolution of the 1950s that influenced political science during the last half of the 20th century. Many of the behavioralists served U.S.'s government during World War II (1939 - 1945), and conducted economic and social analysis as part of the war effort. This marked the genesis of the ground-breaking works of behavioral scholars who emphasized the need to introduce new scientific methods and techniques of science. The tradition of scientific methods in political science was also informed by what is considered by the proponents of scientific study of politic as "Behavioral Revolution.

The idea of behaviorism was the development of research in political science using scientific procedure and methods. According to the major founder of the idea of behavioral revolution, David Easton, there are a number of assumptions and objectives upon which the idea of the revolution was built. These are regularities, verification, techniques quantification, values, systematizations, pure science and; integration. Thus, it could be said that while the discipline of political science originated from the works of ancient philosopher such as Plato, Socrates, and Aristotle, the credit for its development as a scientific discipline should go to leading English and American writers of 20th century.

Indeed, since 1930s, the Political scientists of the Chicago University, popularly known as the Chicago school, had made a clean break with the study of philosophical, historical and institutional approaches and, instead, began to lay stronger emphasis on the observable behaviour of man as a political creature" (Johari, 1979:79). The result of the works of modern intellectuals in political science led to the development of theories, prominent of which are, general system theories, structural-functional analysis, communication group and cybernetic theories.

3.1.3 The Era of Post-behaviourism:

The post-behavioral period is also referred to as the age of action and relevance of the science of politics. Towards the end of the 1960s Political Scientists in the United States became deeply involved in political, social and economic rethinking, especially about the relevance of using scientific theories and tools of political analysis. The goal was to how to employ these new methods and techniques to confront and solve emerging problems and challenges, to prove the continuing relevance of political science to the analysis and understanding of a changing and more complex society. The result of this reawakening was the challenge posed to the behavioralists, and the response to it was the emergence in political science of a paradigm called "post behaviorism".

Since then the focus has been how political science can serve the rich and advanced nations without losing sight of the myriad of socio-economic problems confronting poor countries of the Third world. The emphasis of post-behaviorism is on values such as democratization and good governance; Human Rights in which the engagements of civil society groups now become more prominent; Global partnership and justice between countries in the North versus those of the South; Change in policy focus and priorities in quest of a new world order, rather than mere formulation of public policies or the development of conceptual frameworks, models and theories, that are value neutral.

In order to realize these noble goals, post-behavioralists argue, "knowledge must be put to work" (Varma 1975: 36). In other words, it is not only what you know but what you do with what you know. To be able to serve this purpose Political Science has now developed into different specialized branches and areas of study which include public administration, political economy, comparative politics, public policy, political sociology, political theory, international relations and development administration.

Explain the traditional and the behavioral eras in the development of political science.

3.2   Approaches to the Study of Political Science

From the different epochs in the evolution and development of political science, separate approaches, which also correspond with the dominant theme of each era, also emerged. We will discuss each of these approaches in turn.

3.2.1 Philosophical/Traditional Approach

Under the traditional approach, certain basic questions dominated the attention of such great traditional political philosophers as Plato, Aristotle, Niccolo Machiavelli, Thomas Hobbes, John Locke and Jean-Jacque, Rousseau. They include, what is justice? What makes the exercise of political power legitimate? What should be the proper role of the state in the generation, distribution and regulation of wealth in society? What importance should be given to such political values as justice, natural rights, freedom, obedience and liberty? These questions are understandable since they fall under the normative-philosophical approach, which is the oldest and least scientific approach to the study of politics. The approach is also consistent with the pre-occupation of early scholars with philosophical reflections on those universal political values that were regarded as essential to the just state, and the good citizen. Within the broad traditional school is the other sub-school known as the prescriptive-institutional Approach. It focuses on the discussion of the evolution and operation of legislative, executive and judicial arms, which, respectively, are the institutions for making, executing and interpreting the law. As the approach developed, however, the list of institutions also included political parties, constitutions, bureaucracies, interest groups and other institutions or associations that are more or less permanently engaged in politics. This approach seeks to provide answers to such questions as, what are the historical sources of parliamentary supremacy in Britain. What is the procedure followed before a bill can become law in the United States? By what electoral arrangements are the rulers chosen in a democracy? (Suberu, 1991:4-5)

From the study of these institutions, you as a researcher or student can gain valuable knowledge about their organization and operations make proposals or recommendations for their reforms, and arrive at general conclusion. But it later dawned on the traditional scholars that this approach was no longer adequate for a proper understanding ofpolitical science. For that reason, the approach was criticized for being too static, relying too much on history, qualitative, or based on value judgment, and therefore suffers from objective criteria, since it cannot be scientifically or empirically validated. This was the background to the development of the scientific or behavioral approach.

SELF-ASSESSMENT EXERCISE 2

List the major postulates of the Traditional Approach.

3.2.2 The Behavioral Approach

Proponents of this approach not only emphasize facts over values but also argue that it is the behavior of individual operators in the political theatre rather than the institutions within which they operate, which is the essence of politics. The behavioralists also emphasize the use of scientific and empirical methods in political research, and in fact, believe that political science can become as sophisticated and rigorous as the natural and physical sciences. Behavioralists also call for greater integration of political science with other social science disciplines such as psychology, sociology, geography and economics.

The interdisciplinary perspective of the behavioral approach to the study of political science may be traced to the publication in 1908 of *Human Nature in Politics* by Grahan Wallas and *The Process of Government* by Arthur Bentley. Both books focused on the behavioral and informal processes of political activity, rather than on philosophical approach to highlight the complex role of human nature in political conduct. Bentley used a sociological approach to arrive at the new concept of "groups" in politics. With the end of the First World War in 1918, the behavioral revolution blossomed in the United States, which remained the only country where the behavioral approach is most fully developed. Although a relative decline in the popularity of the behavioral approach was noticed from 1925 up to the end of the Second World War, the approach witnessed a tremendous revival after the war in 1945, and dominated the study of politics through the 1950s.

The major behavioralists in this era included such notable intellectuals as David Easton, Robert Dahl, Karl Deutsch, Gabriel Almond, David Truman and others. The behavioralist approach continued to dominate the study of politics, particularly in the United States until the late sixties when some behavioralists argued that the approach should be revised and refined to accommodate new developments in world politics. This revisionist argument was known as the post behavioral movement and was spear headed by David Easton.

SELF-ASSESSMENT EXERCISE 3

Examine the difference between the Traditional and the behavioral School.

3.2.3 Post-Behavioral Approach

Both the traditionalists and the post behavioralists challenged the major assumptions and premise of the behavioral approach. According to the traditionalist, the assumptions of regularities or uniformities in human behaviour cannot be sustained because human behavior is so complex and fluid in nature that it cannot be subjected to rigorous scientific inquiry. Also due to many forces, including ideology, it is difficult to generalize or make verifications. Rather than offering a mere critique of the behavioral approach, the post-behavioralists sought to remove some of its inadequacies while retaining its more useful assumptions and principles. The four pillars of the post-behavioral approach include:

i).   The need to give greater primacy to the substance or subject of political investigation than the techniques of research and analysis.
ii).   Political science should transcend the social conservatism of the behavioral approach, and instead should concentrate on how to achieve and sustain progressive and constructive change in society.
iii).   Contemporary political science cannot afford to ignore the unfortunate realities of political existence, such as North-South poverty gap and digital divide. Instead, it must address the world crises and conflict situations and contribute towards their resolution.
iv).   The study of politics must be people-centered and be guided by such positive and progressive values of justice, equality and freedom. The idea of value – neutrality in political is not only a myth, but should be discouraged.

SELF-ASSESSMENT EXERCISE 4

Examine the factors that led to the development of the post-behavioral school.

3.3   Methods of Political Science

In over a century of the evolution of Political Science as an academic discipline, a number of methods, which may also be called methodology, have been, and are still being used. Without its own method, Political Science will not qualify as a discipline. But over time the methods are changing in order to cope with new challenges, and as John Mason stated "the man who uses yesterday's method in today's world won't be in business tomorrow". Methods of political science can be seen as the rational working of the mind in the quest for knowledge of political realities. It can also be seen as the technical devices for gathering data. Therefore, the general recognized methods of political science include the following:

3.3.1 Historical Method

The central idea here is that the historical method seeks an explanation of what the past institutions are, in order to appreciate what they have been so as to know their enduring value, if any. It is also pointed out that with the experience of the past one will be able to avoid repeating the blunders of the past. The human race draws upon the experience of past generations, the social heritage, and history being a great teacher of wisdom and a record of experience is better placed to provide this. The historical method has the additional advantage of enlarging mental horizon; improve the perspective and builds up an attitude towards past events. The importance of this method lies in the fact that it not only explains the past it also enables us to draw dependable conclusions. The historical method also supplies us with basic principles for interpreting the future.

3.3.2 Observational Method

This method entails a close observation of the political phenomena under study. This is because things are best studied by direct observation, in politics personal conversation or interactions with legislators and administrators may yield many fruitful results. The observational method involves great difficulties because the authentication of facts is far more laborious in political science than in other subjects. This because the process of government presents many perspectives and one may not be able to see all at a time. What appears on the surface may be but a small part of the reality beneath. Also an observer may confuse the personal or accidental causes, or he/she may be lost in a maze of numerous and conflicting facts. He may also introduce value judgment, which may distort observable facts and becloud his capacity for sound judgment.

3.3.3 Experimental Method

It should be admitted at the onset that "scientific" experimentation as it is done in the natural sciences is not possible in political science. But it should be noted that political experiments are being consciously or unconsciously made at all times. By adopting what is known as counter factual which rely on plausible sequence of historical facts, political scientists can arrive conclusions that are close to verifiable scientific findings. The law of parsimony which enables a scholar to say a lot with few words also allow for precision in presentation of and clarity of expression and analysis. August Comte argues that every political change whether conscious or otherwise, is a sort of experiment. Every new policy, every new law passed and every change made in the political structure and organization is experimental in the sense that such a change is merely tentative or provisional. Political science is therefore experimental not in the sense that laboratory controlled experiments is possible but not only in the very limited sense that conscious and unconscious experimental data from direct observation can be collected, hypothesis formulated and valid political theories formulated.

3.3.4 Comparative Method

This method is employed in the study of political phenomena of different countries and environments using similar or dissimilar political concepts. The objective is to note similarities as well as differences that may exist in circumstance and conditions of the states under comparative studying. This method at the beginning relied on single country study when the focus of political science was predominantly countries of similar culture, in Europe and North America. But when in the aftermath of World War II, countries in Latin America, Asia and Africa also became subjects of comparative political analysis the cross-country approach now became a more acceptable way of distilling facts useful for comparative method.

3.3.5 Philosophical Method

This method is either deductive or inductive. It starts from a premise that it is necessary to construct theories of the state and the purpose of government; while others are inductive method. It thus provides students with the norms or principles based on which political realities can be examined or assessed and suggestions for improvement made. According to Sait, "Philosophical argument develops the intelligence; it impacts resourcefulness and elasticity of mind and it is very doubtful if political science can deal with the multi-various problems confronting it without the benefit of the normative approach inherent in the philosophical method.

3.3.4 Legal Method

This method seeks to benefit from the relationships between politics and the legal process through the institutions created by the constitution and the laws enacted by the legislature for the purposes of maintaining order in the society. Here issues of laws and justice are discussed not as pure affairs of jurisprudence. Rather the state is seen as maintainer of an effective and equitable system of law and order. The notion of the independence of the judiciary, problems of judicial administration and dispensation of justice, though are legal in nature, but they are at the same time of equal concern to political scientists.

This method treats the state not only on its political relevance but also as an organization created equally for the purpose of creating laws and enforcing them. Examples of works based on the legal approach include Jean Bodin and his "Doctrine of Sovereignty, J. Rawls' "A Theory of Justice," and J. S. Mill's "On Liberty." Like the other methods, the legal approach has not escaped criticisms for its highly narrow orientation. This is because law embraces only a single part of a people's life and as such, it cannot cover the entire behaviour of man as a political animal (Mbah, 2007: 28-34).

4.0   SUMMARY

In this unit, we have examined the history, evolution and methods of political science. We observed that political science had its own period of apprenticeship, during which it was fostered by a parent discipline before it matured. We also noted that the approach in the early days of the discipline was rather historical, philosophical than being descriptive, quantitative or scientific. However, today its study has become more rigorous and scientific, combining fluidity in content analysis with precision in its well-developed methodology.

5.0   CONCLUSION

In is over a century of history, the study of political science has developed both in its substance and methods. Though it originated in Europe, political science crossed over to the United States where it witnessed refinements. Presently, the reality of the need to focus on "new" societies outside the West has forced political scientists to embrace cross-country approach to make their studies relevant to Latin America, Asian and African countries,

6.0   TUTOR-MARKED ASSIGNMENTS

1.   Trace the history and evolution of political science as an
      academic discipline
2.   Examine the factors that led to the emergence of the post-
      behavioralists.
3.   Discuss which of the methods used in studying political science
      is most scientific.

UNIT 4   CONSTITUTION AND CONSTITUTIONALISM

1.0   Introduction
2.0   Objectives
3.0   Main Contents
        3.1   The Meaning of Constitution
        3.2   Types of Constitution
        3.3   Importance of Constitution
4.0   Summary
5.0   Conclusion
6.0   Tutor-Marked Assignments

1.0   INTRODUCTION

A constitution is usually a body of rules and regulations; it may be written or unwritten, by which a group of people, a country or an association is to be governed.

It explains the relationship between the organs of government as well as the fundamental rights and obligations of the citizens.

Constitution is the supreme law from which other legislations or enactments draw their strengths. It is also the only means by which the actions of a government and its institutions could be measured or assessed to be legal or *ultra vires*. This unit looks at constitution, its different types as well as its importance within a political system. It also identifies those features that can qualify a government as, or be described as a constitutional.

2.0   OBJECTIVES

At the end of this unit, you should be able to:

- explain what a constitution is and its importance to a
  political system
- assess different types of constitutions, their features and
  characteristics
- critically analyze the significance of a constitution in setting out
  the rules of the game of politics.

3.0 MAIN CONTENT

3.1 The Meaning of Constitution and Constitutionalism

In the modern world, there is no country that does not have a constitution; being a body of fundamental laws by which a country is governed. It is inconceivable that the modern government, with all its complex apparatus can operate without a constitution. Even in the pre-modern societies with its less elaborate institutions, a constitution would still be needed, otherwise the simple task of law making, execution and adjudication would still be less precise, or lack proper delineation, if not problematic. A constitution is therefore a fundamental prerequisite for the political stability, economic well-being and social cohesion of a country. A constitution provides the framework and principles, which governs the organization of government, its institutions, the nation's political philosophy and aspirations as well as the relationships between the citizens and the state.

Literarily, a constitution is the system of laws and basic principles that a state, a country or an organization is governed. A constitution in general terms, is the body of rules which directly or indirectly affect the distribution of power or the exercise of the sovereign power in any nation-state. Classically, it is the collection of principles according to which the powers of the government, the rights of the governed and the relations between the two are adjusted (Bello Imam; 2007:1). The word constitution has been defined in different ways by scholars. A. V. Dicey explained that a constitution is meant to be a document having a special legal sanctity. According to Austin Ranney (cited in Ojo, 1973),"a constitution is a whole body of fundamental rules, written or unwritten, legal and extra-legal according to which a particular government operates".

According to the Black's Dictionary, a constitution is the organic and fundamental law of a nation or state, which may be written or unwritten, establishing the character and conception of its government, laying the basic principles to which its internal life is to conform, organizing the government, regulating, distributing as well as limiting the functions of its different departments/organs. There are two ways we can view a constitution. One can look at it as an "ethno-cultural arrangement" which bring together the way of life of a people. In this sense, a constitution is concerned with establishing a standard by which a people judge themselves and their leaders. In another sense, a constitution can be seen as simply a legal document, which defines the power, structure and the institutional sources corresponding to such power structure.

For example, when the question is asked: What is the basis of the power exercised by the legislature in confirming executive appointments or approving treaties, or that of the judiciary in determining the legality or otherwise of legislations or executive actions? One should look into the constitution to find the rationale. Constitution is therefore a charter of governance; it prescribes how the power of the state is distributed among the institutions in the state, and the process of its amendments. Constitutions define the limits of a government authority, thereby automatically establishing and safeguarding human rights. A constitutional democracy is therefore a form of government, which is regulated by a constitution and whose procedure cannot be altered except by a method accepted by its citizens. Constitutionalism deals with the rule of law. What this suggests is that a government, which a constitution sets up, should conduct itself in accordance with the rule of law and not rule of men. In other words, it must operate according to agreed procedures. S. N. Ray (2006: 109) defines constitutionalism as "a body of normative thought which seeks to realize by means of institutional arrangements, the dominant values..." of a political system. Constitutionalism therefore stands for the principle that the exercise of political power shall be bounded by rules, and with the objective of curbing arbitrariness of political power. Put differently, constitutionalism is government by limitations, both procedural and substantive. And as W. G. Andrew (1961:13) observes under a constitutional government, power is proscribed and procedure prescribed. In short, we can say that a constitutional government is the antithesis to a dictatorship.

Constitutionalism is also based on the principle of shared power. Shared power exists when several independent power-holders or state organs participate in exercise of political power and the power assigned to each organ is subject to reciprocal control (Ray, 2006:110). It should however not to be misconstrued that constitutionalism is restricted to adherence to codified or written constitution. Rather it also embodies respect for the unwritten customs and conventions as practiced in the British democracy.

SELF-ASSESSMENT EXERCISE 1

Explain the difference between Constitution and Constitutionalism.

3.2   Types of constitution

3.2.1 Written constitution

When a Constitution is described as written, it means that the body of rules and regulations by which a country is governed is written or codified in a single document that can be consulted. This presupposes that the Constitution becomes a document through a process that involves (or accommodates the views of) the majority of the people who participate either directly or through their representatives in drafting, debating, reviewing and adopting the contents of the document before it can be regarded as the fundamental laws of a nation. The American Constitution readily satisfies this requirement since it originated from the Constitutional Convention held at Philadelphia in 1878. To some extent, the 1979 Nigeria Constitution can also be regarded as having partially met this requirement since it originated from the Constitution Drafting Committee of '49 wise men' set up by Gen. Muritala Muhammed regime in 1975. The draft was debated by a group of elected Nigerians from each Local Government Areas in the federation called 'Constituent Assembly' that was put in place by Gen. Olusegun Obasanjo in 1975. The document was promulgated into law through a decree enacted by the Supreme Military Council (Ojiako, 1979). The major difference is that unlike the UnitedStates' Constitution that was ratified by nine of the thirteen pioneer states in the country, while that of Nigeria was not subjected to a referendum or a plebiscite.

This is why the preamble "We the people of Nigeria"at the beginning of Nigeria's successive Constitutions since 1979 is viewed in some quarters, as dubious.
We can now identify the salient features of a written Constitution as follows:

1).   It usually contains a preamble at the beginning, which is a statement expressing the essence, goals, aspirations and vision of the people of the country. It is otherwise known the spirit of the Constitution.

2).   It also specify the organs of government, defines their respective powers and their relationships with one another, including the eligibility requirements before individuals can occupy positions in government.

3).   A written Constitution usually states Fundamental Human Rights such as freedom of speech, freedom of association, freedom of movements as listed in *Chapter IV, Sec. 33-45* of the 1999 Constitution of the Federal Republic of Nigeria. It also contains their limitations and safeguards, including the obligations the citizens in a state owe to themselves and the state (Awolowo, 1966).

       Most written Constitutions like those of the USA and Nigeria do contain elaborate procedure for their amendments, which often make most written Constitutions to be rigid from the point of view of the stringent process of altering or changing them. Sec.

9(1-4) of the Nigerian Constitution, 1999 states the cumbersome mode of altering the provisions of the Constitution.

4). The power sharing arrangement is also enshrined in a written Constitution. For instance, the Second Schedule, Parts I and II of the Nigerian Constitution, 1999 contains the Legislative Powers shared among the Federal, States and the Local Government Councils under the Exclusive, Concurrent and Residual powers.

5). The document gives the Federal government the powers to legislate on all items under the Exclusive List; while both the Federal and State governments can legislate onevery item under the Concurrent Legislative List, only the Local Councils have Residual Powers over items not listed under the two Legislative Lists.

It is also noteworthy the consistent addition in the Nigerian Constitution, since 1979, the introduction of a chapter called the Fundamental Objectives and Directive Principles of State Policy which explains the fundamental obligations which are encoded as Political, Economic, Social, Educational, Foreign and Environmental Objectives (See Secs. 13-20, Nigerian Constitution, 1999). However, scholars see the provisions as a façade of honesty because the Constitution did not make it justiciable (i.e. violations by the state cannot be challenged in law court). There are no provisions to guarantee the rights of any aggrieved citizen not satisfied with the performance of a government concerning meeting its Social Contract obligations as enshrined under the sections, can seek legal redress or judicial intervention under the fundamental enforcement.

3.2.2   Unwritten constitution

When we refer to any state as having an unwritten Constitution, it means the guiding principle by which the country is governed is traditionally not set out in a single document. This implies that the fundamental laws according to which the given state is governed are based on *conventions, customs, usages*, etc. The Great Britain is a good example of a country operating unwritten Constitution in her more than 500 years of democracy. The British Constitution is drawn from diverse sources, extending from the 13th century to the present. This means that the British Constitution is more or less a product of a historic evolution that led to the change from absolute to Constitutional Monarchy in 1215.

There was never a period when the people of Great Britain deliberately proposed to make a Constitution but this should not be misconstrued to mean that they do not have a Constitution stating how the affairs of the British people are run. What is important to note is that there is no single book that could be referred to as the British Constitution rather, it is a system of government which has not been written down in a documentary form. In this regard, it must be stressed that some parts of the Constitution are contained in different statute books. The fact that there was no any period in the British history when they actually constituted a constitutional conference for the purpose of making a Constitution makes it impossible to find the British Constitution in a single document. Given its nature, the British Constitution contains not only statutes or Acts of Parliament but also customary laws of the land and conventions, which qualifies to be referred to as Constitution (albeit unwritten). Sources of unwritten Constitution therefore include statutes such as the Magna Carter (1215), Petition of Right (1628), the Bill of Rights (1689), the Reform Act (1832) and the Parliamentary Act (1911), Common Law and Case law, conventions or customs and judicial decisions.

3.2.3 Flexible and Rigid Constitutions

a)   Flexible Constitution

These are the Constitutions whose fundamental laws can be changed or amended by simple majority votes of the members of the Parliament. This form of Constitution is used by small countries that operate a unitary system of government. The amendment can be made in such constitutions by the same procedures used in passing ordinary laws in the parliament. Some of the countries operating flexible constitutions include Great Britain, Ghana during the first Republic, Italy and New Zealand. Flexible constitutions may or may not be written. It is also possible to have a written constitution that is at the same time flexible as shown in the case of New Zealand.

b)   Rigid Constitution

Rigid Constitutions are those that cannot be easily changed or amended because they require special and usually difficult process. This implies that the process of amending such constitution is different from the ordinary law-making process; the process is not only difficult but also complicated. This process is actually laid down in the constitution themselves. Examples of countries with rigid constitutions are Australia, United States of America, Canada and Nigeria. Some reasons have been advanced for adopting the special procedures. It is said that such rigid constitutions should be changed only with proper deliberation; and that such process should give the people, at least through their elected representatives, or via a referendum opportunity to express their views whether a change is necessary or not before such an amendment(s) is made.

The amendment process is therefore made difficult to protect the interests of the people. For example the Nigerian Constitution can only be amended with the concurrence of two-thirds majority of all members of the National Assembly (i.e. the Senate and the Houses of Representatives), and approved by resolution of the Houses of Assembly of not less than two-thirds of all the States in the federation. Another important reason for the adoption of a rigid constitution by a federal state is to prevent the union from disintegration through secession.

3.2.4 Unitary Constitution

A government is regarded as unitary when the national or central government is supreme over other levels of government that might exist in a given state. Other levels of government referred to in the above definition are the local governments or units. The central government has full legal right to over-rule such Local governments. They are not only created by the center, they owe their existence to the center and are subordinate to the national Government. The principle that governs a unitary constitution is Unitarianism. The word 'Unitarianism' means the concentration of political power in the hands of one visible sovereign power; be it that of a parliament or a legitimate dictator. In short, a unitary constitution means that sovereignty is exercised from one source rather than from many sources. It is a unit centre of power, meaning that power emanates from one source only.

3.2.5 Federal Constitution

A country with a federal constitution is called a federation; and its government is referred to as a federal system of government. A federal constitution or system can be defined as a constitutional arrangement in which the powers of government are distributed between the central and component units. In its strict sense, it means the distribution of powers between the government at the federal level and those of the federating or co-ordinate states who are relatively autonomous. This means in effect that the powers being exercised by these component states are distributed along what is known in America as reserved or shared powers, or in Nigeria as Exclusive, Concurrent and Residual powers. From the above definition, we can easily see that a federation is union of autonomous states who have come together to become a larger political entity as in USA or a dis-aggregative federation where a large country is broken into smaller units, as it is the case in Nigeria.

In a federal state each of the component states, like the federal government, derive their powers from the same source- the constitution. This is why Kenneth Wheare (1963), a foremost authority of federalism defined it as a constitutional arrangement in which "neither the central nor regional governments are subordinate to each other, but rather the two levels of government are coordinate and equal." Wheare also set out conditions that can make a federal constitution/system succeed. According to him the component units must be fairly equal in size and population so as to prevent one unit from dominating the other or a combination of two or more units, from dominating the entire federation. As he puts it:

It is undesirable that one or two units in a federation should be so powerful that they can overrule the others and bend the will of the Federal Government to itself. There must be some sort of reasonable balance, which will ensure that all the units can maintain their independence within the sphere allotted to them and that no one can dominate others.

J. S. Mill elaborated on this principle thus:

It is essential in a federation that there should not be any one state so much powerful than the rest as to be capable of vying in strength with many of them combined. If there be such a one it will insist on master of the joint deliberations, if there be two, they will be irresistible when they agree; and whenever they differ everything will be decided by a struggle for ascendancy between the rivals. While the American federal constitution can be said to have met this requirement, the Nigerian federal constitution in the First Republic during which the Northern region bestrode the entire federation like a colossus clearly violated this principle. The states creation exercises undertaken by the successive military regimes in 1967, 1976, 1987, 1990 and 1996 were meant to redress the imbalance inherent in the colonial inherited Nigerian federation. Federalism encourages unity in diversity and a very potent instrument for national integration in plural societies. It is an ideal system for large and heterogeneous countries like the United States, China, Russia and India. It is a delicate arrangement that requires mutual tolerance. In any federal state, the role of the judiciary or the court is vital to ensure that no level encroaches on the other. Its major disadvantage is that it is expensive to run because of duplication of government departments.

3.2.5 Confederal Constitution

Confederation is a league or union of many sovereign states for a common purpose. A confederation has also been defined as that arrangement in which two or more sovereign and independent states agree to come together to have a central but weak government. In other words, the term of a confederation applies to a union of states, which is less binding in character than a federation. Examples of confederal states are the United States between 1776 and 1789, the United Netherlands in 1579, the German constitutions of 1815 to 1867 and 1867 to 1871(before and after the unification of Prussia with other German states).

The features of a confederal constitution include: The states in a confederation would not lose their separate identity through the political arrangement and retain the right to secede. The supreme power belongs to the co-ordinate states. Therefore, the coordinate states dominate the central government; the constitution may not be rigid and the central authority is weak while confederal units are strong and powerful. Judging from the experience of the United States, confederation has not proved to be a successful model, even for those who adopted it after the Americans discarded it in 1789. Other examples of confederacy are the African Union (AU), Economic Community of West African States (ECOWAS), European Union (EU), and the Commonwealth of Nations, to mention a few.

SELF-ASSESSMENT EXERCISE 2

Discuss the major features that distinguish a federal from a confederal constitution.

3.3   Some importance of constitution

A constitution is critical to the understanding of government and how the citizens of a country are governed. It is an instrument for the consolidation of state power. A constitution traditionally explains the powers and limitations of the government in a society. With this, citizens can measure the performance of the government from time to time. Being the embodiment of the general will or the legal sovereign in a state, provisions of a constitution are supreme and superior to any other laws in the land. Every other law in the land must be consistent with the constitution; otherwise, such law or laws shall be null and void to the extent of its inconsistency.

A constitution serves as a medium for setting out the code of conduct or pattern of behaviour acceptable in a given society. More importantly, the constitution in a state usually establishes the direction of the ship of the state by setting out the fundamental objectives and directive principles of state policy. The constitution not only defines the power of each organ, it demarcates the responsibilities of each, thereby eliminate unnecessary frictions or overlapping of functions among different levels or agencies of the government.

A constitution may however not anticipate every situation that may arise. As a result, at the point of drafting not all sentiments, assumptions and aspirations of the people may find expression in a written form. For this reason, a distinction is often made between the letters and the spirit of a constitution. Being a product of human engineering a constitution is not necessarily a perfect document, and may contain some defects or anomalies, or ambiguities, including lacunas that may not come intolight until it is put into practice. At times, judicial interpretations might be required to make such provisions more precise; at other times, an amendment may be necessary to remove ambiguities. In Nigeria, for example, the controversy over the off-shore/on-shore dichotomy and the seizure of the funds due to the local governments in Lagos state were not resolved until the intervention of the Supreme Court. Similarly, the decision by the two chambers of the National Assembly on February 9, 2010, to pass separate resolutions investing the Vice President Goodluck Jonathan with the power of Acting President of Nigeria was one example of finding a political solution to a constitutional crisis. As Senate President, David Mark surmised:

The doctrine of necessity requires that we do what is necessary when faced with a situation that was not contemplated by the constitution...In doing so we have maintained the sanctity of our constitution as the ultimate law of the land (The Guardian, February 10, 2010)

SELF-ASSESSMENT EXERCISE 3

Examine the role of a constitution in a political system

4.0   SUMMARY

In this unit, we have examined the concepts of constitution and constitutionalism and established the fact that we cannot discuss either of the two outside the context of the other. We also discussed different types of constitution, citing examples of countries where each of these constitutions are in operation. The unit finally discussed the significance of a constitution in any political system, where we stressed that a constitution is important not only from the point of view of its written or codified letters which must be adhered to, but its unwritten assumptions, which constitutes its spirit, which must also be respected.

5.0   CONCLUSION

The constitution of any country usually takes its cue from its peculiar circumstances and is also a reflection of the aspirations of its people. It is without doubts the most important document in any political system;

and for this reason, a constitution is sometimes referred to as the ground norm. It is almost a settled principle of political discourse that in a country where there is widespread respect for the provisions of the constitution, a regime of constitutionalism is said to have been enthroned, which in turn will help to generate national consensus and promote political stability.

6.0   TUTOR-MARKED ASSIGNMENTS

1.   Discuss why the description of a constitution as a nation's grundnorm is meant to convey its importance as the fundamental political and legal framework.
2.   Explain the advantages a written constitution possesses over an unwritten constitution.
3.   Critically analyse the view that a federal constitution is better as a devise to promote unity in diversity using Nigeria as your case study.

MODULE 2   POLITICAL IDEAS AND CONCEPTS

Unit 1   The Origins and Theories of the State
Unit 2   The State and Nation-Characteristics and Functions
Unit 3   The Doctrine of Sovereignty and its Limitations
Unit 4   Citizenship, Duties and Rights
Unit 5   Power, Authority and Legitimacy
Unit 6   Major Forms of Government
Unit 7   Democracy as a Form of Government

UNIT I   THE ORIGINS AND THEORIES OF STATE

1.0   Introduction
2.0   Objectives
3.0   Main Contents
      3.1   The Origins and development of the modern State
      3.2   Different Theories of the State
      3.3   Appraisal of the Theories
4.0   Summary
5.0   Conclusion
6.0   Tutor-Marked Assignments
7.0   References/Further Reading

1.0   INTRODUCTION

There are many theories on the origins of the state. Each of these theories gave different reasons why the state came about and became an arena for political activities. This Unit discusses the history and evolution of the state from its early days as city-states until it developed into the modern country-states. It also examines different theories of the state and finally did a brief appraisal of these different theories, under two broad classifications as theory of divinity and theory of destiny.

2.0   OBJECTIVES

At the end of this unit, you are expected to:

- describe the origins and evolution of the state as a political institution
- explain different theories of the nature of a state
- analyse and appraise different theories in order to know which of them fully captures the essence of the state as a political concept.

3.0   MAIN CONTENT

3.1   The Origins and development of the modern State

3.1.1 The City-state

The city-state was an organized society of people living in what the Greeks called "polis." The Greek-city state shared three basic characteristics: small size, love of independence and all-inclusiveness. Appadorai (2004:175-7) has suggested that geographical factor may be responsible for this preference for small size in the days of the Greek city-states. Greece is a land dotted and interspersed with mountains and small valleys, making it impossible for big, linear settlements. Consequently, this natural division encouraged the development of small and separate communities, popularly called the city-states. The Greek city-states also preferred their separate independent status, for reasons that ranged from freedom to practice their different religions, and to pursue different economic activities. By its nature, a city-state was an isolated community that rarely admits of stranger that could possibly pollute its purity. Citizenship status or rights could only be granted by virtue of birth. All the activities of the state: political, economic and social were restricted to the city. According to Aristotle, a city-state must be large enough to be economically viable or self-supporting, but must not be too large as to prevent unity or personal feelings among its members. The city-state also approximates to the Platonic notion of an ideal state: something that is close to the idea of an individual, in which if a part of the body suffers, other parts will feel it and sympathize with the affected part, in the manner of the saying that the "pain of the toe is that of the whole body". However, the city-states could not endure for long and had to collapse because of quarrels and disagreements among them, which peaked when a powerful state in the north, under Philip of Macedon, emerged. In contemporary time the Vatican with its seat in Rome, because it fulfills the features of modern sovereign states of the post 1648 Treaty of Westphalia can be regarded as a city-state.

3.1.2 The Nation-State

The modern state is a nation-state, which is larger than the city-state. Its territory is far bigger and larger beyond the capital city. While in city-states like Athens the citizens are called the Athenians, a name derived from its capital, Athens, this is not the case in a modern state. In a modern state, the citizens of Britain or India are not called Londoners or Delhians, their respective capital cities. Rather they are called Britons or Indians. Other features of the modern country-state include the followings:

(i)   In a nation-state because of its size, only indirect democracy or representative government is possible, unlike in a city-state where participatory or direct democracy is the rule.

(ii)   The modern state also faces more daunting social, economic and political challenges and problems due to its complexity than a city-state.

SELF-ASSESSMENT EXERCISE 1

List the characteristics of a city-state in comparison with that of a nation-state

3.2   Theories on the Origins of the State

There are many theories on how and when the state came into existence. The origin of state has, over the centuries, generated disagreements among scholars. While some have argued that the institution of the state originated from the will of God (the fall of man from the Garden of Eden), others proffered different theories. We will examine these different theories in this section.

3.2.1 The Natural Theory

According to Aristotle, human by nature are social beings; that is they naturally gather and interact among themselves in a community. Beyond the biological necessity for this interaction, human beings also find more fulfillments when they come together socially. This coming together in a community or state is the only way men seek to achieve moral perfection. This therefore makes the state the natural environment in which a man could be truly human, and as Aristotle pointed out; an individual outside the state is either "a beast or a god."

3.2.2 The Force Theory

The force theory has two components: the negative and the positive. The negative conception of the force theory states that the state was created by conquest and force, i.e. by the forceful subjugation of the weak by the strong. A powerful group of bold and cunning men got together and made themselves masters over the rest of the society. They took over the resources of the society, ran it in their own interest, thereby making the rest of the people their servants. The Greek Sophist, Thrusy Machus once observed: "Justice is the interest of the stronger." Marx equally shares this view when he agrees that the conquest band imposes her dominion on the conquered. Machiavelli was also a fanatical believer in force theory when he admonished every prince (leader) to combine force with guile in order to sustain himself in power.

In some respects, it could be argued that Rousseau is also of this view when he argued, "the strongest is never strong enough to always be master, unless he transforms strength into right and obedience into duty". During the inter war years, Benito Mussolini and Adolf Hitler used the force theory to convert Italy and Germany into a police and totalitarian state respectively. Mussolini's idea of a police state is the forerunner of what is today known as Statism. According to him, the State has mystical properties; it is the centre of life, with incomparable purpose and meaning. Just as individual has a personality and a will of its own, the State, Mussolini argued, draw from each developing a personality and will of its own. The will of the state is therefore a measure of values, virtue and wisdom. As the late Italian fascist declared: "The power of the state is total and commitment of the individual must be total...everything for the state; nothing against the state: nothing outside the state".

Likewise, Hitler employed German mythology, elitism, militarism and the concept of a corporate state to foist a one-man power regime in Germany. Hitler declared:

When those with the greatest will to power dominated others, the most perfect possible existence would have been achieved...It is evident that the stronger has the right before God and the world to enforce his will" (quoted in Baradat 2000:251). All the scholars quoted above are all in agreement with Coulumbi who wrote, "Consideration of justice arises between parties of equal strength, and there is no dishonor, but only prudence when the weak capitulate to the poor." MacIves is however one scholar who was opposed to force, since according to him force is destructive violence. "Force does not create right."

History has also shown that though many leaders have acquired power through force (revolution) but not all have been able to keep the power thus acquired through the same means. Due to this origin, the state is sometimes viewed as an evil contrivance that could be resisted in a righteous cause. Harold Laski (1982) was of this view when he described rebellion against the state as a contingent duty of a citizen, especially if it departs from its utilitarian purpose. This conception of the state has therefore given encouragements to revolutionary groups who consider opposition to the state as a worthy and altruistic cause. Thus, in history we saw the rejection of the doctrine of the two swords (Roman Catholic doctrine) by the Protestants, as well as the challenge of the monarchical tyranny by the Republicans.

On the other hand, the positive conception of the force theory developed in 19th century Germany. Rather than being born of, or the incarnate of evil, it is force that is said to dignify the state (Baradat, 2000:52). The concept of "might is right" is meant to legitimize the rule of the strong over the weak. Nietzsche, a prominent member of this school argues that by institutionalizing the power of the strong over the weak the state was doing the right thing; since the weak should be ruled by the strong.

3.2.3 The Divine Rights of the King Theory

This theory states that state is of supernatural authority that was created by God and that God appointed some people to preside over the government of a state on His behalf. In other words, the Chiefs, Emperors, Presidents are said to be anointed orvery close to God, hence the subjects must obey them. Disobeying them means direct opposition to God. The divine Theory was used to justify the rule of monarchs as best exemplified in the rule of the Tudors in Britain. As Appadorai (2004:229) explains "monarchy is a divinely ordained institution"; Kings are accountable only to God only; and non-resistance and passive obedience are enjoined by God." Other example of leaders who have claimed divine right in both ancient and modern governments include the Hindu Maharajahs, who was regarded as the incarnate of the God Krishna, the Egyptian kings reputed to be the son of Ra, and the Mikados of Japan who was said to have carried the claim to divine right to rule to the extreme, when they asserted that they were the incarnations of the sun-God who ruled the entire universe.

3.2.4 The Social Contract Theory

There are many versions of this theory. However, the kernel of the theory is that government came into existence because of a contract between the ruler(s) and the ruled. The understanding is that individuals surrender their rights to rule themselves to the government or a constituted authority, with the hope of getting security and every necessities of life in return. However, why the contract was established or how did it happen, is where opinion differs.

3.2.5 Thomas Hobbes's version

His version of the social contract appeared in his popular book *The Leviathan*. According to Hobbes, in the beginning men were living in a "state of nature" where life was "poor, solitary, nasty, brutish and short." In order to free themselves from the state of nature, which was characterized by selfishness and unbridled desires, men decided to surrender all liberties to one man (the leviathan or king) or an assembly of men. The aim was to transform the state of nature with its insecurity of life and property to a civil society, where peace and order prevails.

This was the origin of social contract or as observed by Hobbes, the creation of the great leviathan. Hobbes wrote the *Leviathan* in 17th Century England to justify the restoration of the Stuart dynasty.

Hobbes' Leviathan was a response to the problem of social order, and was specifically meant to regulate the relations between society and man, and between the sovereign and the citizen. In England of the 17th Century, the forces of absolutism in alliance with Anglican traditionalism were in competition with those of puritan reform that was in league with parliamentary assertiveness. To justify the absolute power he recommended for the monarch or Leviathan, Hobbes had to appeal to natural law (Nisbet, 1973:24). There are also John Locke and J. J. Rousseau's versions of the theory of Social Contract that are different from that of Hobbes' only in emphasis but not in substance.

3.2.6 The Marxian Theory

The basic claim of this theory is that in the beginning, life was not in a state of nature, but was peaceful. There were no selfish people who harbored egoistic interest of appropriating the resources of the society, for their selfish interest, as the society's resource were shared fairly equally by every member of the society. According to the Marxists, this period was known as communalism. However, with the collapse of communalism came feudalism. This period witnessed the emergence of social fragmentation. Some powerful individuals assumed the status of the lords and took over total control over the means of production. Other members of the society were relegated to the status of serfs and were used by the lords as instruments of production on their property. Those serfs had no property of their own and the feudal lords appropriated all that was produced through their labor. During the feudal epoch, the lords formed a government that protected their personal safety and property, and the government kept their serfs under perpetual subjection.

After the demise of feudalism, especially in Western Europe, came capitalism. In the capitalist epoch of development, those who control the means of production are the industrial bourgeoisie and their main instrument of production is the proletariat. In the capitalist state, the government that emerged was that of the bourgeoisie.

Hence, Marx and Engels declared in *The Manifesto of the Communist Party* that the "executive of the modern state is a committee of the bourgeoisie." All laws made in every capitalist state are meant to protect private property or to be specific, protect the properties (banks, industries, cars etc) of the capitalists. The bourgeoisie controls the government and monopolizes the instruments of coercion to protect their private interests. The Marxists further argue that after the demise of the capitalist state, a socialist state will be instituted under which the government will impose its dictatorship on the bourgeoisie. However, after all pockets of resistance by the bourgeoisie and injustice have been completely eliminated, the state will wither away and give way to the dictatorship of the proletariat.

3.2.7   The Family Theory

There are also different versions of this theory; however, there is a consensus among the versions that the state or government started from the family and expanded to the clan or kinship group, to the community and finally the state was created. This means that a single family expanded and the rules made by parents of the nuclear family were transferred to the enlarged family, which later on developed to the level of the modern state. Hence, Maclves has observed that government is continuous by the more inclusive society of a process of regulation that is already highly developed within the family. How this happened is where opinion differs.

3.2.8 Sir Henry Maine and the Patriarchal Theory

Maine has argued vehemently that the modern State or government is traceable to the male decent in every family hence, the evolution of the state is patriarchal in nature. His arguments run as follows: The unit of primitive society was the family in which the eldest male parent was supreme. His power extended to life and death and was as qualified over his children and their houses as masters over his slaves. The single family breathes up into many families, which all held together under the head of first family (the chief or patriarch) becomes the tribe. An aggregation of tribes makes the state. In his own opinion, Milennan believed that the state evolved matriarchal. It is a contention that the primitive group had no common male head and that Kinship among them could be traced only through the woman. That it is only through the women, that blood relationship can be traced and not through men. Hence, he observed that, "maternity is a fact, paternity an opinion."

3.2.9 Evolutionary Theory

This theory considers the state mechanism, neither a divine institution nor as a deliberate human contrivance; but sees the emergence of the state as a result of natural evolution. However, J. W Buress is of the view that the evolution of the state has been due to a gradual and continuous development of human society out of a gross imperfect beginning, through crude but improving forms of manifestation towards a perfect and universal organization of humanity. Sharing this view, conservative British philosopher Edmund Burke (172 9-1777) believed that the state evolved out of a complex set of human needs and that neither these needs nor the characteristics of the state can be totally understood through human reason. He therefore advised against tampering with existing institutions and social relationships because they are the sinews that hold society together.

Furthermore, Greece et al (1976) has observed that the ancient Greeks gave the evolutionary or natural theory of the state, it highest prominence. They had viewed man as inseparable from the state, which they considered not only a necessity for human survival, but also the means whereby man could achieve the "good life." Aristotle assessed that man was "by nature a political animal" who could fulfill himself only through the state and that man outside the state was indeed, not a man at all, but either a god or a beast.

SELF-ASSESSMENT EXERCISE 2

Articulate the contradictions between the Divine Right of the King and the Social Contract Theory.

3.3   Appraisal of the Theories of the State

We can broadly classify the theories discussed above into two; and to use Saint Augustine's terminology, one serving the city of God, and the other the city of man: one spiritual and the order temporal. In its early days, the state was subsumed within the Church. Nevertheless, in the wake of the successive impact of the Renaissance, Reformation and Enlightenment, otherwise called the Age of Reason, the doctrine of the infallibility of the Papacy was challenged. The decline in the primacy of the Church in secular matters was assisted by what was called the indulgences. What is today known as corruption of the leadership of the Church was initially mildly challenged by Erasmus, and later more forcefully by Luther, who led the revolt against the Church and the demand for the separation of the State from the Church. But in spite of its defects or imperfections, until it yielded to the temporal order, the spiritual order from which the theory of Divine Right of the King found its justification, remained an anchor of societal stability.

The rise in secularism-the increasing attention to non-religious values marked the beginning of the emphasis on private initiatives in economic matters, and human rights in politics. Yet, it was realized that individualism if left without control or check could resort to anarchy. Thomas Hobbes, John Locke and J. J. Rousseau, the prime philosophers of this era all agreed that individual should be free, but they disagreed on the definition of freedom, or the limits to be imposed on the exercise of this freedom. Hobbes argued that freedom was possible only when the individuals in society subordinate themselves completely to the monarchs, hence his *Leviathan*. Locke, a liberal believed that freedom could be maximized when the individual was left alone; hence his preference for parliamentary republic, while Rousseau preferred an "infallible" general would, through the democratic process (Baradat, 2000:64-5).

Historically, the Greek city-state where direct democracy was practiced was the highest expression of individualism, at least in political matters. Similarly, Adam Smith's notion of the "invisible hands" in his *The Wealth of Nations*, before the rise of Mercantilism, known today as state's involvement in business foreign trade is its equivalent in the economic realm.

SELF-ASSESSMENT EXERCISE 3

Explain a theory of the state you think will be able to achieve its true purpose.

4.0   SUMMARY

In this unit, we have examined the origins of the state from the period it began from the simple city-state to the more complex and modern country-state of today. We also discussed different theories of the state, and finally did an appraisal of these theories, thereby taking our discussion from the realm of theoretical exposition to a practical level of analysis.

5.0   CONCLUSION

The institution of the state emerged as a political necessity in order to cope with the need of man when he changed from being a wandering into a settled being. Without claiming to be holistic in how they conceived the state, each of the theorists on the origins of the state examined the state from different angles. The correct approach you should take as students is not to accept one theory and reject the others, but how you can reconcile or combine these theories in order to have a more comprehensive view of the state.

6.0   TUTOR-MARKED ASSIGNMENTS

1.   Explain the importance of the theories of State to the understanding of the true purpose of a State.
2.   Enumerate ways by which the challenges of the modern nation-state different from those of the old city-states.
3.   Identify the major Social Contract theories of the state and explain the differences between them.

UNIT 2 THE STATE AND NATION: CHARACTERISTICS AND FUNCTIONS

1.0   INTRODUCTION

In this unit, we will continue our discussion on the concept of the state. We will however proceed from the discussion on the theories of the origins of the state to a more practical level of examining the features and characteristics of the state. We will also discuss the functions of the state, where an attempt will be made to make distinction between the state and government and between a state and a nation/nation-state.

2.0   OBJECTIVES

At the end of this unit, you should be able to

*   explain the meaning and characteristics of a state
*   discuss functions and purposes of a state within a society
*   differentiate between the state, nation and nation-state.

3.1   Definition and Characteristics of a State

Scholars have approached the concept of a state and its definitions from different perspectives. Harold Laski (1982) defines a state as "a territorial society divided into government and subjects claiming within its allotted physical area, a supremacy over all other institutions. In this definition, four elements can be identified: people, territory, government and sovereignty. Although, the words 'state' and 'nation' are closely related, they do not mean the same thing. The term state applies to that political authority which maintains domination over a specific geographical area. It is the means by which the people are organized for the purposes of legal coercion.

To Borlatsky (1978) the state mechanism is usually regarded as "an autonomous entity set-off from the society by a system of norms, rules and prejudices that reflect a certain specialization of labor within the society."

On his part, Marx Weber (1964) defines the state as "a regime or supreme authority, which gives order to all and receives orders from all." Northedge (1971) also gave an international dimension to the state when he defines it as a means by which people are organized for participation in the international system. This conceptualization is closer to that of Woodrow Wilson who defines a state as "a people organized for law within a political community. Karl Marx introduced the ideological dimension to his definition, when a defines the modern state as "a committee for managing the affairs of the whole bourgeoisie"Common to all these conceptualizations is that above all, the state is a political community that recognizes the importance of law in its internal organization and its external relations. A state also functions within a deliberately structured institutional framework. It possesses compulsory jurisdiction over those who live within its territory. Employing his inimitable expressive language to compare the state with other associations, Harold Laski (1982:39) states:

With the state, the case is different. I can dissent from its conclusions only at a cost of penalty. I cannot, in any fundamental way, withdraw from its jurisdiction... It may choose to tax me out of existence... It may compel me to sacrifice my life in a war that I believe to be morally wrong.

"The state," according to Leeds (1981:7), "is a territorial association, an area with a clearly defined boundary within which a government is responsible for law and order." Every person becomes a member of a state at birth and the membership cannot be disowned but citizenship can be transferred through naturalization. The state has a monopoly of coercive powers over every person domicile within the defined territory. This implies that all individuals and groups living within the state are subject to its authority. The authority exercised by the state is usually defined by the constitution, which provides for the institutions of government that are necessary to ensure internal stability and external security. For any polity to be regarded as a state, it must have the following fundamental elements: *population; defined territory; government and sovereignty*. These characteristics differentiate a state (properly so-called, e.g. Nigeria, USA, etc.,) from a state (a component unit in a federation, e.g. Lagos, New York, Illinois, etc.,) and such other sociopolitical institutions like a nation, a society, etc.

Since the state is an artificial person, it operates through an agent called ' the government' which is an administrative institution capable of resolving conflicts between groups within the society by making enforceable decisions without necessarily the use of force. Although, government as the agent of a state, is that body which exclusively exercises the legitimate use of force in making regulations and in enforcing its rules within the given territorial boundary. However, the allegiance and loyalty of the citizenry in a state is to the state but expressed it through the agents of the state - the government. In addition, states seldom apply force to maintain its authority as the threats of sanctions or punishments, which constitute the basis of justice, are sufficient to obtain obedience.

One of the main purposes of government is to minimize or eliminate likelihood of any challenge to the state's authority. Otherwise, the possibility of internal conflicts and instability that might lead to the failure of the state is imminent. It should be noted that the government (in this context) is a narrow concept, a sub-structure within the superstructure of the state; since the state includes both the government and the governed while government is only the machinery through which the state realizes its purpose. In addition, sovereignty is the characteristic of the state and not of the government even though the government exercises sovereignty on behalf of the state. Another distinction is that while the state is relatively more permanent than government, government is temporary and changes more frequently. It is however possible that one state may dissolve into several other states like the former Soviet Union, which broke into fifteen new states. Yugoslavia also split into six after a civil war, which led to the disappearance of the country from the world map while Czechoslovakia dissolved into two states - Czechs and Slovak.

The random and arbitrary ways in which frontiers are superimposed on the world map means that states vary enormously in their sizes, mineral deposits, access to the sea, vulnerability and cohesiveness. Part of the authority of the state came from other states recognizing its sovereignty, i.e. the state's ability to exercise supreme power over its citizens without external interference. In international law, there are two kinds of recognition; *de facto* and *de jure*. De facto recognition of one state by another is given when a state agrees that another is able to exercise proper governmental control over its territory. De jure recognition is given, if the recognizing state thinks that the method by which the government in the other state was formed is in accordance with the accepted constitutional traditions and procedure of that state.

The table below summarizes the relationship between the state and the government:

The State	The Government
State is the principal	Government is the agent
Life expectancy is permanency; Lives in	Life span is ephemeral/temporary; It changes hands periodically
Membership includes every	Only a few employed or elected are
Existence is abstract	Exists in concrete terms, could be seen
Power and authority are	Exercises delegated powers and
Powers and authority are absolute	Powers and authority are limited by the constitution
States are not different in nature	There are different forms and types of
Membership is compulsory	Membership is optional

SELF-ASSESSMENT EXERCISE 1

List the major characteristics of a State and a government.

3.2   Functions of the State

The state evolves for the sake of life and continues "for the sake of life" (Aristotle). The end of the state is therefore ethical. As Newman puts it: "the state exists (according to Aristotle) for the sake of that kind of life which is the end of man. When the state by its education and laws, written and unwritten, succeeds in evoking and maintain in vigorous activity a life rich in noble aims and deeds, then and not till then has it fully attained the end for which it exists". The ethical end of the state is subordinated to convenience in Locke's view. His concern is not with the 'good' but with the 'convenient'. This is the preservation of the people's property-which is Locke's general name for 'lives, liberties and estates'. The manner these natural rights is preserved is therefore the purposes of political society; and the exercise of power by government is conditioned by that purpose (Appadorai, 2004) Adam smith (1723-90) in his *The Wealth of Nation* (1776) laid down the following as the three duties the sovereign must attend to:

1.   The duty of protecting the society from violence and invasion of other independent societies
2.   The duty of establishing an exact administration of justice 76

3.   The duty of erecting and maintaining certain public works and certain public institutions for the society

In contemporary language, these three functions are the maintenance of internal law and order, defense of a state independence, sovereignty and territorial integrity, efficient administration of justice and provision of public good and infrastructural facilities. Writing on the purpose of the state, Laski says the state is an organization that enables the mass of men to realize social good on the largest possible scale.

SELF-ASSESSMENT EXERCISE 2

Identify and discuss the purpose of the State

3.3   The Class Character of the State

The assumption of statehood by most nations obscures the urgent fact that the state is only one, however, important, of the various groups into which society is divided. In the opinion of Harold Laski (1982:235), the state is, in its daily administration, the government; and the government may lie at the disposal of a special interest and it is essential it consult with the various groups if the will realized is to represent a just compromise between competing wills. In other words, Harold Laski was indirectly affirming Marxist's notion of the state, which states that a state expresses a will to maintain a given system of class relations.

Indeed, the territorial character of the sovereign nation-state enables a small fraction of its members to appropriate its power for its own ends even against the interest of their fellow citizens. It does so by the use of its supreme coercive power to that end. In a feudal state, law is made to serve the interest of the owners of land, the reason it embodies is their reason; the general end of society it seeks to fulfill is its conception of what that general end should be. Similarly, in a capitalist society, the owners of capital will similarly determine the substance of the law predominantly. However, it also reflects the interest of the society as a whole. Therefore, the idea of equality before the law within a state is meaningless, unless such society is a classless one.

The question arises whether the citizens always obey the state. What are the reasons for peoples' obedience? Is it out of fear, habit, consent or utility? No doubt, in some degree it is all of these. In a feudal state, the serf had no option but to live as the feudal lord decrees because it was upon such obedience that his livelihood and existence are guaranteed. In a capitalist system, the coercive power of the state is always at the disposal of the ruling class to compel obedience, thereby enforcing their will. The difference between a feudal and capitalist society is that while obedience was usually secured in the most crude, even cruel ways in the former, In the latter, the pretence to democracy makes obedience to state voluntary and freely given since it is assumed that the state authority are exercised in the interest of the generality of the people. The veneer of participation of all citizens is thus reinforced by the freewheeling principle of the capitalist system, which in a reality is a contraption to promote the interest of a few.

SELF-ASSESSMENT EXERCISE 3

Differentiate between the feudal and capitalist society in terms of obedience to the state.

3.4   The Concept of Nation

The term nation is often used as a synonym for state or country. This is not technically correct. Indeed the concept of a nation is not political, but sociological. A nation can exist even though it is not contained within a particular state or served by a given government. A nation exists where there is a union of people based on similarities in linguistic pattern, ethnic relationship, or cultural heritage. Although the German people make up the bulk of the population of Germany, but the Austrian and Dutch are also Germanic. For thousands years until the creation of the state of Israel in 1948 the Jews maintained a national identity without a state of their own. In addition, between 1797 and 1919, the Polish state ceased to exist as a political entity but the Polish nation survived.

 It is common to talk of one's nationality or one's state of origin as if the two are interchangeable or synonymous. One can belong to a state without belonging to the nation or one of its constituent nations. Conversely, one can belong to a nation and not the state in which it is located. For example, it is possible to find members of Yoruba nation outside the traditional home states (Southwest of Nigeria) of the nationality. It is also possible for a nation to live across many states (e.g. Igbominas in Kwara and Osun States of Nigeria). It can also be transnational like the Hausas and Yorubas in some West African countries. Similarly, a Nigerian living in London can be a British citizen without being an Irish, English, Scot or Welsh. In effect, while the state is a political entity with sovereignty, a nation is a group of people bound together by the sentiment of nationality - race, culture, religion, language, history. However, the state has monopoly of coercive force but a nation lacks such element power. Only the states not nations, are recognized and represented at the international for a such as the United Nations, African Union, International Monetary Fund, Arab League, etc. Nigeria is a nation of about 250 nations (ethnic nationalities) that make up the 36 states of the federation. Similarly, the United States of America became a nation that made up 52 states after the independence war with the Great Britain.

SELF-ASSESSMENT EXERCISE 4

Differentiate between the concept of a state and nation

3.5   The Nation-State

The nation-state has become the principal form of political organization among modern people. In the past Tribes, City-states, Empires and Feudal barony were known. Indeed, in political terms, part of the definition of a modern society is that it is organized into a nation-state. The term nation symbolized the unity of a people around which people unify and through which they identify themselves and assess political events. So strong is the peoples' identification with the nation-state that political leaders often need to claim that a particular act is in the national interest to satisfy many citizens that the policy is justified. Many scholars have listed specific pre-conditions such as a common language, religion and ethnic heritage before a nation-state can emerge. This is not strictly valid. Switzerland, for example with four official languages and Belgium with two, are good examples of nation-states. The United States is ethnically diverse, and yet remains a model of a nation-state. Obviously common language, religion and ethnic origin will help create a nation-state, but it is not mandatory as the U.S.'s experience as a successful nation-state has shown.

However, what is essential is that the people feel that they share deeply significant element of a common heritage and that they have common destiny for the future. Groups of people who are completely different have been brought together by accidents of geography, military conquest, local and external political rivalries. But they can see themselves as one, or members of a nation-state to the extent to which they co-operate in common enterprise such as self-defense against external enemies, acceptance of similar concepts of political authority and legitimacy and see their future as being bound up with each other and being willing to accept this prospect.

SELF-ASSESSMENT EXERCISE 5

Describe what qualifies a state or nation to become a nation-state.

4.0   SUMMARY

In this unit, we have examined the concept of the state in a practical sense by defining it and outlining its features and characteristics as well as its functions. We attempted to bring out the differences between a state and nation/nation-state. We also explained that a state is a political while a nation is sociological concept, and that a state does not automatically transform into a nation-state unless certain integrative or adhesive conditions are met.

5.0   CONCLUSION

The state is usually the primary arena within which several nations in the modern world always look towards to find opportunities for better fulfillments. Many factors have made the idea of multi-lingual and multi-national states compelling for both the developed countries of the West and developing countries, especially in Africa. Among others, the need to meet the increasing social, economic and political challenges of the modern world, in case of the former; and the historical factor of colonial partition, in the latter case. But for every society, no matter its level of development the state will continue to play vital roles of serving as instrument of promoting community building and national integration.

6.0   TUTOR-MARKED ASSIGNMENTS

1.   List the characteristics of a state, emphasizing the conditions that   can assist the promotion of a state to a nation-state.
2.   Enumerate the difference between the conventional and Marxian conception of the state.
3.   Distinguish between Government, State and Nation.

UNIT 3   THE DOCTRINE OF SOVEREIGNTY AND ITS LIMITATIONS

1.0   Introduction
2.0   Objectives
3.0   Main Contents
    3.1   Definition of the concept of sovereignty
    3.2   Types of sovereignty
        3.2.1   Legal sovereignty
        3.2.2   Political/Popular sovereignty
        3.2.3   External Sovereignty
    3.3   Criticisms and Limitations of Sovereignty
4.0   Summary
5.0   Conclusion
6.0   Tutor-Marked Assignments

1.0   INTRODUCTION

Sovereignty is a very important concept in political science and it is the foundation for the survival and existence of the state in both its domestic and external affairs.

This unit sets out with a working definition of the concept of sovereignty; it discusses its relevance as well as different types of sovereignty. The Unit also presents criticisms of sovereignty both from the theoretical and practical point of views, as well as from its limitations as a philosophical and political concept.

2.0   OBJECTIVES

At the end of this unit, you should be able to:

- define the concept of sovereignty, its different types and relevance as apolitical concept
- explain relevant criticisms of sovereignty with a view to bringing to light that it can only be applied in a modified form
- discuss the recent developments on the international scene in relationship to the concept of sovereignty.

3.0   MAIN CONTENT

3.1   Definition of the concept of sovereignty

Sovereignty may be defined as the power of a state to make laws and enforce the laws with all the coercive power it can employ without any external interference. It is that characteristic of the state by virtue of which it cannot be legally bound except by its own will or limited by any power than itself. The modern states claim to be sovereign, and to be subject to no higher human authority. It issues orders to all and receives order from none, and its will is not subject to any legal limitation of any kind. The French writer, Jean Bodin (1530-96), introduced the theory of sovereignty into the study of political science. He, it was who postulates that, "If the state is to live there must be in every organized community some definite authority not only itself obeyed, but also itself beyond the reach of authority." Harold Laski corroborates Bodin's definition when he concludes that when we discover the authority, which gives commands habitually obeyed but itself not receiving them, we have the sovereign power in the state. By these characterizations, in an independent political community sovereignty is determinate, absolute and illimitable.

Sovereignty is a supreme power of the state over her citizens and subjects, itself not bound by the laws. Scholars who have helped to develop the theory of sovereignty include Thomas Hobbes, John Locke, J. J. Rousseau, and Jeremy Bentham. According to Hobbes, sovereignty is absolute and located in the ruler, his premise being the social contract. Locke did not use the term sovereignty at all; in so far there was a supreme power in his state, it lay with the people; but normally it was latent. Rousseau maintained that sovereignty belonged to the people; it could be exercised only in an assembly of the whole people. Government was but the executive agent of the general will: it had no manner of sovereignty. The sovereignty of the people of Rousseau was as unlimited just as morally is unlimited. It is limited by the possibility of resistance, and there are conditions under which resistance is morally justifiable. Bentham urged the necessity for the sovereign to justify his power by useful legislations to promoting "the greatest happiness of the greatest number."

Within the domestic environment, the sovereignty of the state is located in, or exercised by persons or institutions. In a monarchical system, sovereignty is located in the king except where that king is a constitutional monarch like in Britain, where the law obliges or compels a division of sovereignty among several institutions of the state, with the parliament in obvious supremacy. In a republican democracy like the United States, a number of institutions also shares sovereignty, where the President occupies a primacy. In most modern democracies, one of the principal institutions involved in the exercise of the sovereign power of the state is the Legislature or Parliament, which has powers to make laws that are binding on all including the lawmakers.

Others are the Executive, which has constitutional responsibility for enforcing or executing the laws while the Judiciary, which has the power to interpret and adjudicate disputes arising from the constitution and the law. There has been a great deal of academic debate on whether sovereignty is determinate or illimitable. It is not worthwhile to reopen such a debate here but the important thing is to know what sovereignty denotes and connotes. First, in every state there must be a sovereign, the sovereignty must be clearly located, his commands are laws and within the sphere of law, as Hobbes said there is no such thing as an unjust command. Second, such laws or commands may oblige the subjects to do, or to refrain from doing, certain things and failure to comply attract penalty. Therefore, sovereignty is located in that individual, group or association which is obeyed without question by the rest of the people in a state.

SELF-ASSESSMENT EXERCISE 1

Describe the defining characteristics of the theory of sovereignty.

3.2   Types of sovereignty

The most common distinction is that which is made between legal and political sovereignty, on one hand, and internal and external sovereignty on the other. Legal and political sovereignty can be subsumed within internal sovereignty, while external sovereignty is relevant to, and applicable in the conduct of international relations. However, in the present interdependent world when bridges of cooperation among states are fast replacing barriers or divisions, the distinction is no longer of strict relevance, but merely serving academic purposes or analytical convenience.

3.2.1 Legal sovereignty

John Austin is the foremost exponent of legal sovereignty. For him the state is a legal order in which the sovereign is determinate and exercises ultimate power. He admits that a sovereign may act unwisely or dishonestly, but for the purpose of legal theory, the character of its actions is not important. This view is similar to the popular saying in Britain that "the King or Queen can do no wrong." But since a constitutional Monarch like it obtains in Britain operates within a legal or unwritten conventional milieu, legal sovereignty connotes also the power of the legislature to make laws, or that of constitutive and regulative laws of the state as symbolized or permitted by the constitution, which is the supreme law.

It is also plausible to ague essentially that legal sovereignty resides in the constitution. Although the legislature can review, amend or even mutilate the constitution, it can only do so in accordance with the same constitution. This makes the idea of legislative sovereignty to be limited or suspect. In any case, the legality or otherwise of a legislation can be challenged in the court of law whereas the constitution cannot. All that can be done to the constitution in the court of law is to interpret it in a way to make its provisions less ambiguous and more precise. In this sense, we can only talk of legal sovereignty, which means the supremacy of the constitution.

3.1.2 Political/Popular sovereignty

It is also possible to talk of political or popular sovereignty, which in fact refers to the ultimate power of the people. It is often argued that the people make up the polity and all constitutions are, or ought to be reflections of their preference, culture and institutions. By popular/majority will, they also enthrone and can also displace or remove governments. Consequently, in discussions of sovereignty it is tempting to suggest or conclude that the people are sovereign. Nevertheless, in practice the impact of the people in the process of law making or drafting of constitutions is minimal, if not nil. Most legislators hardly consult their constituents before vital decisions are made, recall procedure is cumbersome to be applied as a check on recalcitrant legislators, while the electoral process, particularly in Third World nations hardly reflect popular will. For these reasons, we must be cautious in placing too much hope on the strings that the political sovereign can pull. This is why Laski dismisses as an abstraction, attempts to equate popular sovereignty with public opinion, especially when we do not "know when public opinion is public and when it is opinion."

In the modern state, it is therefore an illusion to suggest that the people are sovereign. Only the very active, powerful, aggressive or interested, actually get to exert any influence on the constitutions, institutions of state or the workings of government. The mass of the people cannot only govern in the sense of acting continually as a unit, more importantly; the business of the modern state is far too complex to be conducted by perpetual referenda. John Chipman Gray confirmed elitist rule when he declared that the real rulers of society are undiscoverable. For the most part, constitutions and regulative rules emerge from the manipulation, compromises and conflicts of powerful minorities. The majority often concedes through apathy, indifference or ignorance their right to influence public policy. Thus, while in theory; the people are sovereign, in practice; it is the constitution that is sovereign and the operators who exercise this sovereignty.

However, it is possible for the people to be mobilized to assert themselves and influence the legal sovereign (constitution and parliament) in such a way as to suit their interest or desires. Such occasions however are rare. They occur only in moments of crisis when there is need for radical changes. In short, sovereignty is meaningless in the absence of power; that is power to enforce laws. But as others have argued power is neither necessary nor sufficient for the exercise of sovereignty. What is central and necessary is to earn the obedience of the people, which ultimately enhances the possession, and exercise of authority.

3.1.3 External Sovereignty

Sovereignty is the central organizing principle of the international system. It means essentially supremacy and separateness of states as legal or political entities with power to control others and regulate not only their internal affairs, but also their external or foreign relations. The state is sovereign within a defined territory and enjoys equal status with others, which have the same attribute. The importance of Hugo Grotius in the development of the theory of sovereignty is that he emphasized external sovereignty, i.e. the independence of the states from foreign control. Sovereignty is therefore used in reference to states, which are autonomous of any other entity. Although, membership of international organizations is voluntary, States willingly join because they consider such participation to be in their enlightened national interests. States can also decline the jurisdiction, or refuse to abide by the judgment of the International Court of Justice (ICJ) as the United States has severally done with its optional clause or that of the International Criminal Court (ICC) by refusing to ratify its Statute. This is still within the exercise of a state external sovereignty.

The idea of sovereign state in diplomatic history had its roots with the signing of the Treaty of Westphalia in 1648. After the Thirty Years War the sovereign state emerged from the bloody clash to vindicate the supremacy of the secular order against religious claims. And since then states have been guarding jealously their sovereignty, equality and territorial integrity. From the 1815 Congress of Vienna,through the 1919 Versailles Peace Treaty, the San Francisco Conference of 1945, which gave birth to the Charter of the United Nations, the 1961 Vienna Conference on Diplomatic Immunity to the 2000 Rome Treaty of the

International Criminal Court, the notion of sovereignty of states, has been preserved.

SELF-ASSESSMENT EXERCISE 2

Discuss ways in which legal sovereignty different from political sovereignty.

3.3   Criticisms and Limitations of Sovereignty

There are several criticisms of the theory of sovereignty. First, in the view of Sir Henry Maine sovereignty it is not applicable to undeveloped communities, among whom custom is the king of men (Appadorai, 2004). Second, sovereignty assumes that the state is the only association. This is not true according to the pluralists who recognize the existence of other non-political associations like trade unions that grow naturally, have a will of their own and possess personality distinct from that of the state. They also have members who find fulfillment within such bodies. Third, in a federal state it may not be easy to determine or locate sovereignty in one source giving the origin, cooperative and dual character of most federations, which often compel distribution of powers among levels of government. But a caveat to this criticism is that even in federations efforts are being made to build overarching national consensus. As Laski puts it, "The will of the state must be all or nothing. If it can be challenged, the prospect of anarchy is obvious." It was this realization, which made Abraham Lincoln in the United States between 1861 and 1865, and Yakubu Gowon of Nigeria from 1967 to 1970 used federal might to suppress rebellion by the secessionist states to keep the federation intact.

Fourth, the sovereign must habitually observe certain principles or maxim. For example, it is unthinkable that the Queen in Parliament will ignore established age hold conventions that hold the British society together. Fifth, in a democracy, it is almost a truism that the legal sovereign should bow to the political sovereign. Thequestion then is: if sovereignty is determinate, how can the people or the electorate where popular sovereignty rest, satisfies this requirement? Sixth, while it is conceded that the law of the sovereign is a command, yet the state cannot make laws that offend the historical and sociological milieu of a society, otherwise the sovereign may risk resistance, or even rebellion. Seventh, to say that there is no law beyond the reach of the sovereign is to strain the definition to its limit, as the sovereign cannot tax private property without the consent of the owner. As Laski warned, "Men will sooner part with their souls than with their possessions."

The concept of absolute, unlimited sovereignty did not last long after its adoption, either domestically or internationally. The growth of democracy imposed important limitations upon the power of the sovereign and of the ruling classes. The increase in the interdependence of states restricted the principle that might is right in international affairs. Citizens and policymakers generally have recognized that there can be no peace without law and that there can be no law without some limitations on sovereignty. They started, therefore, to pool their sovereignties to the extent needed to maintain peace and prosperity. For example, the North Atlantic Treaty Organization, United Nations, European Union, African Union and ECOWAS Charters, which modern states are signatories and respected, serve as limitations on their sovereignty.

In spite of these criticisms, sovereignty remains a valid legal and political theory. In those levels of society in which obedience is habitually rendered by the bulk of society to an authority or superior who is independent of any other superior, the obedience is so rendered because this authority or superior is regarded as expressing or embodying what may properly be called the general will. This sovereign does not exercise an unlimited power of compulsion since his power is dependent upon his conforming to certain convictions that the subjects consider to be in line with the general interests. The sovereign is able to exercise the ultimate power of getting habitual obedience from the people because of what the people stand to gain for so doing. The consent is not reducible to the fear of the sovereign; rather it is a common desire to achieve certain purpose towards which obedience to law contributes.

The Austinian conception of sovereignty which emphasizes a determinate person or body of persons with sovereign power is therefore not without qualifications. It only suggests common interest, a common sympathy, and a desire for common object, which we call the general, will, and which the people believe is embodied in the sovereign. The foregoing is what Harold Laski (1982:62) had in mind when he wrote of a modified view of sovereignty. In his characteristic inimitable way, he wrote: "If the state is to be a moral entity, it must be built upon the organized acquiescence of its members. But this demands from them the scrutiny of government orders; and that, in its turn, implies a right to disobedience." Therefore, will, not force, is the basis of the state.

On the limitations of the concept of sovereignty, there has been a great of debate on its relevance when it comes to the arena of international relations. Scholars like John Herz, J. Rosenau, R. Cooper and Karl Deutsch have argued at one time or the other that sovereignty has become obsolete. Herz's position is that nuclear weapons have undermined the isolation and separateness of states making them vulnerable to decisions outside their control. Rosenau's concept of cascade interdependence argues from the point of view that other states, forces or agencies that intrude into the decision-making process of another, thereby undermining its supremacy and separateness. Karl Deutsch premised his argument on the rise of hegemonic powers, which have the capacity to impose their will on others and exercise such power without authorization and often with impunity. This was the case when the United States in 2003 invaded Iraq, topped Saddam Hussein's government and forcefully imposed its coercive will on the country, an action that amounted to virtual extinguishing of Iraq's sovereignty.

This reality has reduced the sovereignty of smaller states, making them live at the mercy of powerful ones as it happened when Kuwait was overrun by neighboring Iraq in August 1990, until her sovereignty was restored in January 1991 after the intervention of the United Nations backed, US led Allied Forces. For similar hegemonic, imperialist or economic reasons countries such as Vietnam, Grenada, Panama, Afghanistan, Georgia, at one time or the other, were at the receiving end of the ambitions and manipulations of super powers like USA and the former Soviet Union, now Russia. Joseph Nye Jnr. (2000:177) also wrote extensively on the subject of economic interdependence of states, how it seriously undermines or reduces the capacity for independent action on the parts of sovereign states.

SELF-ASSESSMENT EXERCISE 3

State the major criticisms and limitations of the theory of sovereignty.

4.0   SUMMARY

This unit examines the concept of sovereignty and stresses its importance as an organizing principle of the state in both its domestic and external relations. The point was made that sovereignty belonged to the state and not the government; the latter being a mere agency of the former. We also emphasized that despite the views of the classical theorists a modified theory of sovereignty is the one that is realistic in the modern state in which its ultimate purpose is better served only if the interests of its citizens are maximized.

5.0   CONCLUSION

In spite of the limitations of the concept of sovereignty, it retains its relevance and vitality in politics at both the domestic and international levels. Within the state system, supreme power is located in the major political institutions or the constitution. Although the ability of a state to govern may be influenced by extraneous forces, it is uncommon to find any state, which is not managed largely based on its constitution. Therefore, from the issues raised in this unit and recent developments in the world of sovereign states though we may concede that sovereignty is no longer absolute, yet they have by no means eliminated the formal independence of states, their separateness and the ability of governments in those states to exercise sovereignty on behalf of their people.

6.0   TUTOR-MARKED ASSIGNMENTS

1.   Define the concept of sovereignty from the perspectives of different scholars.
2.   Critically analyse the possibility of identifying a sovereign under a federal system of government
3.   Explain the limitations to sovereignty and how it could be sustained.

UNIT 4   CITIZENSHIP RIGHTS, LIMITATIONS AND PROTECTIONS

1.0   INTRODUCTION

In this unit, we will examine human rights and duties as reciprocal concepts in citizenship. The unit begins with the discussion of the origins and identification of various human rights, in their two broad categorization into natural and civil rights. The unit continues with a discussion of the limits to these rights as well as government's obligation to safeguard them as a pre-requisite before the citizens can justifiably be required to perform their duties to the state.

2.0   OBJECTIVES

At the end of this unit, you should be able to:

- explain the origins meaning, categories and limitations of fundamental human rights
- discuss ways by which rights can be fully enjoyed and protected
- enumerate the importance of these rights as reciprocal to the performance of the duties of the citizens to the state.

3.0   MAIN CONTENT

3.1   Definition and Limitations of Human Rights

Human rights can be defined as those privileges enjoyed by the citizens of a given states. The privileges are usually defined and enjoyed within the bounds of the law i.e. the law of the country. In written constitutions these rights, the limits to such rights and the protection accorded them by the government are specified. In other words, human rights are spelt out in written a constitution of modern democracies and protected by the government being a charter of the United Nations. The protection of these rights calls for two forms of action on the part of the government. Government is forbidden to do a series of things to the individual in order to preserve his/her rights and the government is obliged to perform certain obligations to the individual purposely to preserve his/her liberties against which the citizen can enforce the rights through judicial process.

Historically, the origins of human rights can be traced to the American Declaration of Independence of 1776, which proclaimed right to life, liberty and pursuit of happiness, the French Declaration of the Rights of man in 1789, the European Convention of Human Rights and the 1948 Universal Declaration of Rights. Many political scientists have written and said a lot on fundamental human rights. Its most influential exponent perhaps was the English political philosopher John Locke, who wrote that the obedience to the commands of a given government is for only one reason, and that is to secure the personal rights to life, liberty, and property that naturally belong to all men equally, simply because they are all human beings. In the Nigerian constitutions since 1963 Republican Constitution, there has been a Chapter devoted exclusively to the provisions on Fundamental Human Rights.

Chapter IV of the Constitution of the Federal Republic of Nigeria, 1999 guarantees the citizens' Fundamental Human Rights in the following section of the document thus:

Sec. 33:   Right to life
Sec. 34:   Right to dignity of human person
Sec. 35:   Right to personal liberty
Sec. 36:   Right to fair hearing
Sec. 37:   Right to private and family life
Sec. 38:   Right to freedom of thought, conscience and   religion
Sec. 39:   Right to freedom of expression and the press
Sec. 40:   Right to peaceful assembly and association
Sec. 41:   Right to freedom of movement
Sec. 42:   Right to freedom from discrimination
Sec. 43:   Right to acquire and own immovable property
             anywhere.

The First amendment to the American constitution also lawfully secures freedom of speech and of peaceful assembly. The Fourth secures the citizen that his house shall not be searched except upon a warrant while the Eight legally secures citizens against excessive bail (Laski; 1982:103). In the unwritten British Constitution, however, there has been no general proclamation of rights but each of a series of important rights has been achieved because of a particular struggle in history, and its maintenance today depends on the working of the law.

In short, whether a country operates a written or an unwritten constitution, there are Fundamental Human Rights guaranteed for the individual citizen and protected by law. These Rights include right to life, freedom of association, freedom of speech, freedom from slavery, freedom of religion, freedom of assembly, freedom from unlawful imprisonment and right to private life and property. Right to life, for instance is the foundation on which other rights are based. This is why murder and suicide are punishable under the law by capital punishment, even when sanctioned by the state, for many reasons, including the sanctity of human life remains a controversial subject. However, when we say human rights are inalienable it does not imply that they are not without qualifications. This means in effect that there are some rules guiding these various rights or liberties.

Limitations to Human Rights

Fundamental Human Rights are not without limitations since it is obvious that absolute right is as good as no right at all. A Citizen should know that his/her rights ends where that of others begins. For example, you have a right to stress your hands the way you like but you should not box or hit anybody with your hands in the process, otherwise you may be charged to Court with assault and battery by the aggrieved person. Law of libel is a limitation to the freedom of speech and writing if it defames or impugns the integrity of another person. The freedom of assembly could be lawfully curtailed in order to prevent a breakdown or law and order. Freedom of movement could be withdrawn by the state during emergency period, people may be asked to stay indoor from dusk until dawn to observe a curfew. A citizen who is mentally challenged could be 'arrested' and 'detained' in a psychiatric hospital for treatment, against his/her wish to roam the street. Citizens could also be conscripted into the Army and sent to the war front to defend the state, which may serve as a limitation to his/her freedom to life (Sec. 33). Restrictions on and derogation from fundamental rights are contained in *Secs. 45(1)(a)(b)(2)&(3)* of the 1999 constitution of the Federal Republic of Nigeria. Human rights are said to be inalienable, yet without detracting from this view it is still a fact that the only part of the conduct of any one, for which he is amenable to society, is that which concern others.

Liberty and Equality

Liberty does not mean freedom to do one's will. This is a negative conception, which suggests absence of restraint, which the rich prefer. The presence of government will make this definition of liberty impossible. Liberty means the maintenance of equal opportunities for all citizens. Liberty therefore is a positive thing. It does not merely mean absence of restraint. Regulation is required since citizens cannot live together without common rules. For example, a citizen's liberty is not endangered if he is refused permission to commit murder. So also is observing traffic regulation. To compel obedience to them is not to make a man un-free.

Where restraint becomes an invasion of liberty is where the given prohibition acts to destroy productive endeavors (Laski; 1982).

Liberty, therefore, is never real unless the government can be called to account, especially when it invades rights. In his Essay on Liberty, John Stuart Mill wrote: "That government is best which governs least." There are three aspects of liberty. The first is private liberty. This means the opportunity to exercise freedom of choice in personal life, like in religious beliefs. The second is political liberty. This is the citizens right to participate in the political activities of his country-right to vote and to stand for elections and to criticize the government-A citizen must find no barriers that are not general barriers in the way of access to position of authority. The educational system must not be structured such that children of rich or well-born men are trained to imbibe habit of authority while the children of the poor are trained to habits of deference. The third is economic liberty. This means security and the opportunity to find reasonable means of livelihood. As argued by Laski (1982) where there are rich and poor, educated and uneducated, we find always masters and servants. Therefore, liberty cannot exist without equality.

Economic liberty also means democracy in industry or what is called equal economic opportunities. Freedom can therefore not exist in the presence of special privilege, since there is no liberty where the rights of some depend upon the pleasure of others. Equality does not mean identity of treatment. There can be no ultimate identity of treatment so long as men are different in want, capacity and need. It implies, fundamentally a certain leveling process, and the provision of equal opportunities for all, which also depends on the training we offer to citizens. For the power that ultimately counts in society is power to utilize knowledge; and disparities in the ability to use that power. In the final analysis, political equality is never real unless it is accompanied by economic equality since political power is the handmaid of economic power.

Types of Liberty

Personal	Political	Economic	Domestic	National	International
Freedom of choice on strictly private	Right to take part in state affairs	Right to gainful employment	Responsible and respectable position of family	Freedom from colonial subjugation (independence)	Renunciation of war
Health security, personal honour	Right to exercise franchise	Freedom from want	Freedom to enter into matrimonial alliance	Exercise of loyalty and patriotism	Abandonment of the use of force
Freedom of thought, expression, movement and faith	Right to free supply of news and information dissemination	Right to produce, distribute and consume goods	Responsibility of parents for seeking development of family members		Pacific settlement of disputes among nations
Freedom to use enjoy private property	Right to fight for free and fair elections	Workers' right to participate in the management of industry			Limitation on the production of armaments
	Right to send petition to the government	Establishment of industrial democracy			
	Right to support or oppose government policies and actions				

Types of Equality

Natural	Social	Political	Economic	Legal	International
All are born free, no discrimin at ion the ground of sex, religion, race, language,	Equality of rights and opportuniti es subject to genuine ground of discriminat io n	Equality of participati on in the political process	Equality in the resource allocation/di st ribution	Equality before the law	Equality of states. No discrimination on the basis of demography, geography, economic or military potential
		Universal adult suffrage	Provision of protection for the minority groups' interests	Equal protect of law for all	Eradication of social evils such as slavery, child abuse/trafficki ng, drug trafficking, etc
		Open leadership recruitmen t through credible, periodic elections	Control of private sector through social policies	Equality of access to justice through a low cost and without unnecessa ry delay	
		Free press and mass informatio n media			

Source: Johari, J. C., (2007:194 & 210)

SELF-ASSESSMENT EXERCISE 1

List and explain different types of liberty and equality you know

3.2   The State and protection of liberties

Every state is measured by the amount of liberties and rights that it obliges her citizens. The state is not simply a sovereign organization with the power to get its will obeyed, it must safeguard rights by preventing unlawful invasion of rights and ensuring that a citizen's right stops where another's begins. Harold Laski (1982:131) made this delicate balance clear: "It is a state, for instance which can prevent the Roman Catholic Church putting a man to death for heresy; but it cannot force the Roman Catholic Church to surrender the dogma of Papal infallibility." Also a state cannot demand allegiance from its subjects, expect in terms of what that allegiance is to serve. Indeed, the state character will be apparent from the rights that, at any given period, secure recognition. Any given state is therefore torn between rights that have been recognized and rights, which demand recognition. Rights, in fact, are those conditions of social life without which no man can seek, in general, to fulfill himself. Since, the state exists to make possible that achievement, it is by maintaining rights that its purpose may be served.

For example, rights such as freedoms of speech, association assembly, religion are rights either equally applicable to all citizens without distinction or not applicable at all. Freedom of speech is only limited by the law of libel, or slander, as a constraint on the freedom of the press. Opinion, in the view of Harold Laski (1982:119) may be penalized if it is held to involve disorder. But in order to ensure that rights are respected by the state authorities, it is imperative to ensure in the constitution the principle of separation of powers, and the system of checks and balances. In the opinion of Harold Laski (1982:104) the more independent a judiciary, the more adequate are the safeguard of rights. However, he added a caveat that since the executive ultimately appoints the judiciary, its independence is rarely final. Indeed, separation of powers merely acts as checks upon the expansion of each authority's allotted sphere into another; it does not determine the quality and the extent of the power that are allotted.

It is therefore not enough for a state to make verbal commitments to respect human rights; statutory and institutional frameworks are required to back or safeguard them. In the United Kingdom, for example, there is a special precaution against unlawful imprisonment. A citizen unlawfully imprisoned can proceed against whoever imprisoned him through the writ of *Habeas Corpus*. This is an order from a judge of a Law Court requiring whoever is being detained to be produced before the court on a given date. The effect is that any person unlawfully detained, can obtain his release or trial at the earliest time possible. In Nigeria, if a citizen is unlawfully arrested, he is entitled to receive compensation; and if lawfully arrested, he enjoys the right to defend himself accordingly. In a similar manner, a citizen can bring a writ of *Mandamus* from a Law Court to compel any level of government to perform its constitutional responsibility. A citizen can also protect his/her liberties by seeking either *interlocutory* or *perpetual injunctions* from a Law Court, to compel a stay of action that may violate his/her rights.

The essence of safeguards of human rights is to prevent governments from invading citizens' rights or the latter from engaging in acts of lawlessness, which are capable of throwing the state into chaos. It is also to ensure that individuals can perform their lawful duties without fear of oppression and victimization. A government, which deprives its citizens of these fundamental rights, would have lost its legitimacy to remain in office. Hence, John Locke's remark that:

The great and chief end... of men uniting into commonwealths, and putting themselves under government, is the preservation of their property (i.e. their natural right); and when a government fails to preserve these rights and thereby cease to serve the end for which it was created, the citizens have the right – indeed, the duty, to overthrow it.

Law is therefore an important condition of rights. But laws can either help or destroy liberty because laws can positively provide equal opportunities or negatively curtail freedom. A. V. Dicey once argued that the more there is one (law) the less there is the other (rights). The independence of the judiciary is achieved by providing for appointment or removal of judicial officers through a due process to ensure job security; and payment of their salaries/allowances from the Consolidated Revenue Fund. Other measures to protect Human Rights from encroachments are: i) A written constitution in which the rights and obligations of citizens are set out in a lucid and unambiguous language. Citizens are aware of these liberties and measure of defending them if violated.

ii)   Existence of *Ombudsman* - a Public Complaints Commission, through which any aggrieved citizen, can seek a redress against the state or any of her agencies.

iii)   A free press that will report and disseminate information, as well as educating the citizenry about government policies and its implications on their rights and liberties.
A democratic government also helps to safeguard human rights, because democratic institutions such as the Senate, House of Representatives and State Assemblies are composed of elected people who are representing different constituencies in the federation. They protect members of their constituents through public hearing, motions and bills to protect citizens' rights.

iv)   Quick dispensation of justice is another element in protecting rights and liberties of citizens. As the saying goes, "justice delayed is justice denied," the judicial process should not only be fast but should also be accessible to the poor through a reasonable cost of litigation.

SELF-ASSESSMENT EXERCISE 2

Enumerate ways of protecting your liberties in your country.

3.3   Importance of Human Rights to Citizenship

In any given state citizens are endowed with rights because without them they may not be able to function optimally, or perform their civic obligation to the state. Put differently, rights are corollaries to duties. For example, a man has not only the right to work; he has the right also to be paid an adequate wages for his labor. To live citizen without access to the means of existence is to deprive him of that which makes him perform his basic civic obligations, or function in the interest of the larger society. As Laski put it; "there must be sufficiency for all before there is superfluity for some". The state also provides for the right to property if what a citizen owns is commensurate to his efforts, or can be shown to be related to the common welfare. However, a citizen cannot justifiably own directly because of the efforts of others; or if the effect of such ownership is a power over the life of other. Indeed, there is an income below which no man can be allowed to fall if he is to be himself as a decent citizen.

The state in civilized modern state accords right to education top priority, since the citizen who lacks it is bound to be the slave of others. He will not only live a stunted being, but also fails to rise to the full heights of his personality. If citizenship means the contribution of one's instructed judgment to the public good, a citizen without basic education will not be able to make informed choices. Related to this is a right to political power. Every adult citizen has the right to indicate the person he desires should be elected. If the body of voters is limited, the welfare realized usually excludes that of the persons excluded. But just as those who choose cannot be drawn from any special class in a state so also, those who are chosen cannot be members of a limited section only.

SELF-ASSESSMENT EXERCISE 3

Outline the benefits that citizens can derive from respect for human rights in a country

3.4   Citizenship, Duties and Obligations

Just as every citizen has rights which are entrenched in the constitution and are to be protected by the state, so also the constitution requires of every citizen certain duties and obligations. This implies that for every privilege there is corresponding responsibility.

3.4.1 Definition of citizenship

Citizenship means membership of a given state. A citizen is a person who is a freeborn of a state. Put briefly, a citizen is an individual who has full political and legal rights in a state. Under international law, every nation has the right to determine how a person can acquire her citizenship. Chapter III of the Constitution of the Federal Republic of Nigeria, 1999 stipulates ways by which a person could acquire citizenship of Nigeria. Aristotle defines citizenship as the rights to rule and be rule. Ways of acquiring Citizenship may be by birth; place of birth blood/descent, by marriage, registration, naturalization or by conquest.

3.4.2 Duties of a citizen

Duties are the responsibilities the citizens owe not only to the state but also to themselves for effective functioning of the state as well as the harmonious relationships between the individuals and the social groups within the state. If it is responsibility of the state to protect the rights of the individual citizen, the citizens also have some duties to perform in reciprocity. The organic theory of the state states that without the individual performing its functions, (duties) the state cannot function. The duties that citizens owe to the state include, but not limited to: Obedience and unalloyed loyalty to the state - this encompasses respect to the national flag and national anthem; Payment of tax as and when due; Obedience to traffic laws and highway codes; Serving in the military if required during emergency period; Non-interference with other citizens' right.

3.3.3 Obligations of a citizen

These are civic responsibilities that directly or indirectly contribute to an effective government and the avoidance of those acts, which may tamper with the rights of others. Good citizens, for example, are expected to exercise their voting rights during elections and citizens or voters who decide not to vote on the day of election are actually contributing to the election of an unpopular government. Therefore, it is politically obligatory for every citizen having the right to vote to exercise his voting right during elections and it is equally necessary to resist the reign or the ruling of an unpopular government by constitutional means i.e. by removing such a government through the exercise of his/her voting right. Every citizen owes it an obligation to obey the government provided the government is good, and not to deprive others of their rights. It is also obligatory on a citizen to assist the law enforcement agencies in the detection and prevention of crimes in the society.

SELF-ASSESSMENT EXERCISE 4

Explain the relationship between citizenship, rights, duties and obligations.

4.0   SUMMARY

In this unit, we have defined and examined various categories of human rights. We also observed that in spite of their character as inalienable; these rights are not without qualifications or limitations. We also stated that a citizen could only enjoy his rights fully on the condition that he knows his limits under the law and perform his duties. Where this is the case, the state acting through the government is to ensure that a citizen's rights are fully guaranteed, protected and safeguarded.

5.0   CONCLUSION

Human rights are assumed to be within the sovereignty of every state. But presently international norms about human rights continue to develop, because what happen within one state may spill over to others. This is why international organizations like the United Nations and non-governmental international organizations like the Amnesty International are increasingly leading the crusades that states must respect human rights. The UN Commission on Human Rights, The Human Rights Watch and conventions on genocide, tortures, racial discrimination, women and child rights are global initiatives meant to promote respect for human rights. In the world today, because of the danger that the poverty gap poses to order and security, it appears there is more emphasis on promoting economic rights, rather than pre-occupation with political rights, even though the two are related.

6.0   TUTOR-MARKED ASSIGNMENTS

1. Describe the constitutional and institutional safeguards available in your country for the protection and enforcement of fundamental rights
2. Explain the relationships and differences between fundamental human rights and the fundamental objectives and directive principle of state policies.
3. Discuss the axiom "Eternal vigilance is the price of liberty" is meant to emphasize citizen's participation in protection of human rights.

UNIT 5   POWER, AUTHORITY AND LEGITIMACY

1.0   Introduction
2.0   Objectives
3.0   Main Contents
    3.1   The meaning of the concept of Power
    3.2   Attributes and elements of National Power
    3.3   Differences in the concepts of Power/Influence and
        Authority/Legitimacy
4.0   Summary
5.0   Conclusion
6.0   Tutor Marked Assignments

1.0   INTRODUCTION

Power is an important concept in political science, as it is well
known that all struggles in politics is centered on the acquisition
and retention of power. In this unit, we attempt to provide meaning to
the concept of power, its characteristics and elements and its
importance in political relationships. The unit makes further
attempt to make distinctions between related concepts of authority and
influence.

2.0   OBJECTIVES

At the end of this unit, you should be able to:

- define the concept of power and know its characteristics,
  elements and importance
- differentiate between the concepts of power, authority/legitimacy
  and influence
- discuss the necessity for the state to put limitations on the
  exercise of power by the political leadership.

3.0   MAIN CONTENT

3.1   The meaning of power

The concept of power features regularly in political discourse. For this
reason, it is often said that power is to politics what energy is to physics.
Power is also often used interchangeably with power and influence. But
in spite of the apparent relations, the three concepts have different

meanings. We will however focus on power in this unit and defer the discussion on the others till section 4.3 hereunder. Power, when used in a socio-political context, is the ability by Mr. A to get Mr. B or other people to do what they would ordinarily not have done. This ability may be a derivative of possession of either: a gift, trust/goodwill, supernatural power, public office or any other coercive superiority over others.

However, the more precise meaning of power necessarily involves the concept of coercion. Power is the ability or capacity to get other people to do ones wishes, with or without their consent; that is, whether they like it or not. This may be as a result of social, biological or economic relationship e.g. between father/children, sponsor/beneficiary, political godfather/godson. Similarly, possession of a monopoly of weapon or agents of death e.g. armed robber/victim, armed security official/unarmed civilian. It can also be a group of armed military officers forcing their way into power. Power is invariably tied up with superior quality or capability. This is where power is different from influence. It is important we make this distinction at this stage in order not to mistake power for influence. Our concern here is primarily power, even if we recognize that other forms of power-economic in particular- may have almost decisive impact on political power.

3.1.1 Political power

Max Weber defines power as the "probability that one actor within a social relationship will be in a position to carry out his own will despite resistance." The corollary of this is that power relationship is said to exist when A makes B to act in a manner he wants him to act, regardless of B's wish. Inherent in the power relationship therefore is the element of sanction, coercion and the use of physical force. While sanction is the drive of fear of punishment by A and B, coercion refers to compulsion by A of B to carry out his wish, and the use of physical force involves the threat by A to harm B. It should however be noted that the power relationship does not necessarily involve the use of physical force, although elements of sanction and coercion may be in the background, which help to enhance the credibility of power.

Political power is the capacity to affect another's behaviour by the threat of some forms of sanction. The greater the sanction, or the more numerous the sanctions, the greater will be the political power. The sanctions may be either negative or positive or a carrot and stick approach. Thus, a political leader may acquire compliance with his wishes by promising those who support him with wealth or honors, or he may threaten to deny such rewards to those with both. The penalties for opposing the holder of political power may be extreme, such as imprisonment or even death. These latter penalties are usually reserved for the state, and those who control the state's apparatus often wield the strongest political power.

However, it is the fear of these coercive penalties that provokes the obedience, not the coercion itself; indeed a too frequent use of these penalties may be an indication of the weakening of that political power. Nonetheless, if those who claim authority lack the power to enforce their will, they cannot rightly claim authority. Political power is important not because it is an end in itself but because it is a means to an end. Power can serve as an instrument both for empowerment and for domination. For this reason, scholars have warned against the possibility of misuse or abuse of power, since according to Lord Action, "power corrupts and absolute power corrupts absolutely"

SELF-ASSESSMENT EXERCISE 1

Attempt a good and concise definition of power

3.2   Attributes and Elements of State Power

Power in politics can be understood to mean the sum total of national capabilities, including the tangible and intangible resources of a nation. Power is also a political resource, which encompasses the sum of the various attributes of a state that enable it to achieve its goals. The characteristics or attributes of power include the following:

3.2.1 Attributes of Power

3.2.1.1 Power is dynamic

Power being exercised by a state changes from time to time, and is never static but dynamic. Before 1991, the Soviet Union was a Super Power, but today the country has ceased to exist. Indeed, its successor state, Russia is far from assuming status in the world today. Until the turn of the 19th Century, Britain was perhaps the most powerful country in the world, with colonial possessions across the globe. Today Pax Britannica is now history with leaving the United States as the most powerful country in the world today, in all the dimensions of power.

3.2.1.2 Objectivity and Subjectivity of power

Objective power consists of assets that a state actually possesses and has both the capacity and will to use. On the other hand, subjective power depends on perception, and in some cases, appearance may be more important than reality. It is easier to assess the contribution of the tangible than the intangible elements of power to a nation's power matrix. Tangible elements are easily more measurable and thus objective than intangible power, which is less precise and thus, subjective.

3.2.1.3 Power is relative

Power can best be perceived in relative than absolute term. Power therefore becomes meaningful when you compare the power a nation wields in a particular period with another, or when actor A is compared to actor B. For example, we cannot say Nigeria is powerful in absolute term, except we specify in comparism to whom, or compare power of a country between one period and another.

3.2.2 Elements of national power

3.2.2.1 Tangible Elements

The tangible elements of a national power include military capabilities, economic strength, natural resources, demographic or population, strategic location, etc. These elements however interrelated and need some qualifications. Military capability consists of both conventional and nuclear powers and without it a state may not be able to defend her territorial integrity, which is a vital attribute of a state. Similarly, a country with a weak economic base may not be able to acquire military weaponry or sustain political stability. The size and quality of a country's population may constitute either an asset or liability and this may have serious implications on national power. For instance, Nigeria is respected in the international community among others, because of her heavy population, which has psychological effects in the global system. It is also not enough for a country to have huge natural endowments, its power will remain qualified if it has to rely on other nations for technology to explore or exploit the resources. A country that is strategically located along the coastline will command more respect or wields more power in the international politics than a landlocked country. A landlocked country that has no territorial waters has to depend on foreign country(s) international trade through the sea. This will make such a country vulnerable to external control.

3.2.2.2 Intangible elements

The intangible (or soft power) elements of national power include culture, attraction of ideas, ideology and institutions. This form of power does not require any form of coercion. The power a state like the Vatican wields today in the world, especially among the Catholics is principally because of religion. Beyond her tangible oil wealth, Saudi Arabia occupies a prime of place in the Muslim world on account of the religious intangible of the city of Mecca, located in the country. There is no doubt that the widespread acceptance of western values, including western idea of liberal democracy, and even the near acceptance of the capitalist ideology as the orthodox route to development, is a huge accretion to the power Western nations, especially the United States, exercises in the world today.

SELF-ASSESSMENT EXERCISE 2

Explain the elements of a state's power that you consider most important

3.3   Differences in the concepts of Power/Influence and Authority/Legitimacy

3.3.1 The Concept of Authority

Authority has a relationship with power but it is distinct from it in one important respect. It is based on rules. It is common to define authority as legitimate power but this may be misleading because it gives the impression that coercive power is necessarily illegitimate. When coercive power is used or exercised by the state it is legitimate. While a definition of authority needs not exclude the concept of power, the two concepts are not synonymous. Authority is the consequence of the acknowledgement of power. This may also be misconstrued because it is possible to accept or acknowledge other people's power as "a fait accompli," but this would not necessarily confer legitimacy on such force. For example, if one surrenders a property to an armed robber, it is an acknowledgement of power but it does not confer authority or legitimacy on that power.

A more acceptable definition will be one that sees authority as legitimate power, that is, power derived from accepted rules and exercised with the consent of the people. Thus, authority rather than brute force is better understood when power is seen as a right to issue command and have them obeyed willingly. We can therefore regard authority as a form of power. It is different from the form of power exercised by A over B in order to get B to do what he could never had wish to do. Rather, it is a form of power derived from approved procedures of political culture, which enable the office holder to act in certain ways to affect predictably and in anticipation, the behaviour of others. In a democracy for example, there is compliance with the executive directives of the president of a country not for his individual person but because the office holder has been freely given a mandate to rule through procedures acceptable to them. Compliance therefore, is voluntary and in support of a system, which the people hold in high esteem. In the same token, when a legal system is established, it is recognized and obeyed by the people voluntarily regardless of whether a particular law is wrong or right. Thus, authority has been described as legitimate power because it commands voluntary obedience. This is in sharp contrast to the power structure of superior-subordinate relationship in which the command of the superior usually takes precedence. Herbert Simon (cited in Bello-Imam, 2008) described the circumstances surrounding the exercise of power as Sanctions of Authority" The sanctions are not in the sense of punishment, but as a means of explaining why subordinates carry out commands from their superiors. It is said that in a republic it is not power that creates obedience, but authority.

3.3.2 The concept of Legitimacy

Max Weber identifies three major sources of authority. These are not three different kinds of authority but only different sources of authority .These are the traditional, legal rational and charismatic. Traditional authority derives from long standing traditions and common acceptance of the sanctity of traditions and usages. This takes the forms of respect for the monarchy or chief or Oba/ Emir, respect born out of the inheritance of the status of one's parent and exercise of authority conferred on that status. Legal rational authority is legitimated by the supremacy of the law. The exercise of such power is accepted as legitimate because it derives from institutionalized rules, which confer and circumscribe the right to give command and have them obeyed. In the legal rational situation, such a right derives from rules, e.g. constitutions status whereas in a traditional situation the right derives from customs, usages and acceptance of common antecedents.

Charismatic authority derives from persons of exceptional qualities who are accepted and obeyed as leaders. Such qualities include heroism, power of oratory, intelligence, power of healing or prophecy, etc. Charismatic authority often derives from a common acceptance or a voluntary submission to the perceived competence or superiority or simply charisma of a leader. Leaders such as Mahatma Gandhi of India, John Kennedy of the United States Chief Obafemi Awolowo, Sir Ahmadu Bello and Muritala Muhammad of Nigeria are examples of leaders who, during their lifetime, possessed charismatic qualities that endeared them to the people of their countries.

3.3.3 Influence

Influence is the ability to intrude into other people's decision-making process. It involves, largely, the capacity to make ones presence felt in other people's minds. Influence can be exercised without power, although it can be conferred by power. Also important is the fact that influence can also acquire the intensity of power. This happens when somebody's influence is so overbearing that others have no choice but to take account cognizance of the person in their decision-making. The distinction between power and influence can only be made in terms of the form of the relationship between actor A and B. At the same time, it would be correct to say that power relationships also connote influence, since both concepts express the relationships between A and B. Power and influence are inseparable.

3.3.3.1 Forms of Influence

Influence has been identified to take several forms, which can be classified into two categories - manifest and implicit influence. Manifest influence is said to exist where B is able to anticipate **A's** wants. For example, if A wants outcome **X**; and if as a result of A's action, **B** attempts to bring about X, then A exercises manifest influence. On the other hand, if **A** wants outcome **X**, then although **A** does not act with the intent of causing **B** to bring about **X**, if **A's** desire for **X** causes **B** to attempt to bring **X**, then **A** exercises implicit influence over **B** (Dahl, 1984:42-5).

3.3.3.1.2 Means of Achieving Relationship of Influence

The relationship of influence could be achieved through several means or a combination of them. The means according to Robert A. Dahl (1984) include trained control and persuasions which could be rational, manipulative or inducement.

3.3.3.1.3 Trained Control

Influence through trained control takes the form of prior persuasions and inducement aimed at manipulating actors' behaviour in the required direction in compliance with appropriate cues and signals.

3.3.3.1.4 Rational/Manipulative Persuasion

Rational persuasion is influence borne out of truthful information and rational communications. The relationship of influence derives from an appeal to the emotion of conscience of **B** concerning the genuineness of the subject over which he is being influenced. On the other hand; manipulative persuasion is achieved through half-truths and falsehood presented to **B** by **A**.

3.3.3.1.5 Inducement

This is an influence relationship in which there is the offer of reward in order to prevent anticipated action. Examples include offer of wage rise and the threat of strike action or improved student's amenities and students' boycott lectures.

SELF-ASSESSMENT EXERCISE 3

Identify the differences between authority and influence.

4.0   SUMMARY

In this unit, we have defined power, its features and indices as well as significance in a political system. We also differentiated between power, authority and influence. We underscored that while power involves coercion, authority connotes voluntary acceptance and submission to control. We however conceded that it is not unlikely to see people use the two concepts interchangeably in ordinary discussion, leaving the strict distinction between the two to academic discourse.

5.0   CONCLUSION

The concept of power, influence and authority express relationships among human actors, and the distinctions that could be made between these concepts is only in the extent of variance in the form of relationship. In other words, there is no hard and fast rule in trying to differentiate between these concepts, outside the form which relationships take among human actors. They are generic items and hence Robert A. Dahl used "the concept of influence" to embrace them all, including related concept such as control, persuasion, might, force and coercion.

6.0   TUTOR-MARKED ASSIGNMENTS

1.   Differentiate between the concepts of power and authority.
2.   Explain the imports of Lord Action's famous quote: "Power corrupts and absolute power corrupts absolutely"
3.   Discuss the circumstances under which influence could assume the status of power.

UNIT 6   TYPES OF POLITICAL SYSTEMS

1.0   Introduction
2.0   Objectives
3.0   Main Contents
    3.1   Monarchy
    3.2   Aristocracy
    3.3   Theocracy
    3.4   Totalitarianism/Dictatorship
4.0   Summary
5.0   Conclusion
6.0   Tutor-Marked Assignments

1.0   INTRODUCTION

In the history of political organization, citizens have lived under different types\forms of government. They range from monarchy through aristocracy to democracy, among others. However, what is of utmost importance and a central subject of political enquiry is that the form of government a state or country operates considerably affects freedom of the individual citizen. This Unit discusses forms of governments, their merits and demerits and how each of them has developed over the centuries until the modern times when democracy has now become the most popular and acceptable form of government.

2.0   OBJECTIVES

At the end of this unit, you should be able to:

- analyse the characteristics of various forms of governments.
- discuss how political organizations have evolved from   one to another form of government.
- explain which of the system of government is for the safety of the rights of the citizens.

3.0   MAIN CONTENT

3.1   Monarchy

The first and earliest form of government is monarchy. Simply, it is a form of government that is headed by individual who is not subject to legal limitations, or who does everything according to his own will. Monarchy is a type of government headed by a Queen a King or an Emperor. Examples are the United Kingdom and the Kingdom of Saudi

Arabia. A constitutional monarchy is one that is subject to legal limitations like that of the United Kingdom, in contradistinction to the absolute monarchy of Saudi Arabia. However, it should be noted that hereditary monarchy is the normal type but elective forms do exist also. Therefore, the essence of monarchy is the personification of the majesty and sovereignty of the state in an individual. Monarchy can bring about a stable political system; it is also a natural institution, where obedience to the king is seen as obedience to God.

Britain probably offers the most contemporary example of a country operating a monarchy. Indeed, British monarchy had evolved from the days of absolute monarchy of the Tudors to that of the constitutional monarchy of Queen Elizabeth. This transition was a consequence of the Puritan revolt that erupted between the King and the parliament. It was later resolved bloodily after what came to be known as the Glorious Revolution in 1688. The characteristics of monarchy include the following: monarchy is an age-long form of government; the government of the country is in the hands of a king, emperor or queen; it is a type of government that is based on hereditary pattern. In some forms of monarchy, e.g. absolute monarchy, the ruler has no constitutional limitation. In some monarchies, e.g. constitutional monarchy, the ruler is under checks by the constitution.

A monarchical form of government has some advantages: Monarchy can bring about a stable political system; it is a natural institution where obedience to the king is seen as obedience to God and thus promotes total loyalty to the state. A stable political system and can best be secured only where supreme authority is vested in a single ruler. Monarchy could be adopted to make for emergency situation when the state requires undivided loyalty of the people to the government of the day. In a monarchical system decision-making is faster since the monarch need not consult anybody before necessary and urgent decisions are taken.

Monarchy helps to harmonize different interests and prevent social strife. In some circumstances, the king may serve as the protector of the people at large, from the tyranny of the few. Where a hereditary kingship has been in existence for a considerable time like in Britain it may be unwise and unnecessary to abolish it. Democratic principle can be grafted into as it was done in Britain with admirable success. The disadvantages of monarchy include the following: Good intentions, ability, industry are not hereditary. Therefore, a monarch could be a bad leader. A monarch could also be despotic to keep the people weak so that they may be unable to resist him.

Forms of Monarchy-Broadly, there are two types of monarchy: Hereditary and Elective. Absolute monarchy: This occurs when there is no established constitutional authority to check the king's power. The king rules as the head of government and head of state. Examples are Frederick the Great of Russia, the Queen of England, Louis XIV of France, before the French Revolution. Hereditary monarchy can be found in countries such as Britain or even in the old Oyo Empire where the Alaafin of Oyo or the Hausa Fulani Empire, where the Sultan of Sokoto were regarded as the personifications of the state. Despite the incursion of foreign rule and the displacement of traditional rulers under the post-colonial dispensation in many African states, monarchy has survived even with diminished power and authority. The phrase "the king reigns but do not rule" aptly captures the present position occupies by monarchs in contrast to the days of unlimited absolutism.

3.1.1 Constitutional Monarchy

The power of a constitutional monarch is regulated by the constitution. The monarch can promulgate only those laws that are agreed upon by the resolution of the elected parliament as in Britain. Also, he or she is bound to respect not only the spirits of the constitution but also the laws of the state. He assents to only those laws that passed by the elected parliament. Britain is a good example of a constitutional monarchy.

SELF-ASSESSMENT EXERCISE 1

Describe the differences between absolute and constitutional monarchy.

3.2   Aristocracy

Aristocracy is a government that is led by the best citizens; the quality, which marks out the aristocrat from others, is virtue: moral and intellectual superiority. Because the aristocrat possesses these qualities in abundance, he only assumes leadership; he does not need to explain or justify his claims to superiority or leadership positions. In short, his deeds, not his words attest to his preeminence. In the view of Appadoria (2004), any time an aristocrat is compelled to justify his power, "it will be proof that his position is crumbling."

The distinctive qualities which characterize an aristocracy include noble birth (aristocracy of family), culture and education (aristocracy of priest or of scholars), age (aristocracy of elders), military distinction (aristocracy of knight), or property (aristocracy of landowners). Several Scholars have tried to justify aristocracy as a form of government. Carlyle said "it is the everlasting privilege of the foolish to be governed by the wise' Rousseau also contended that it is the best and most natural arrangement that the wisest should govern the many. Montesquieu equally noted that aristocrats usually possess the great virtue of moderation. This quality also makes them to be cautious in their leadership role in order not to ignite resistance from the rank of the masses, who have the advantage of number.

Plato indeed likened democracy to a mob rule, and argued that a few people with high quality, if allowed to rule could do better for a society. Although Aristotle was not as cynical about democracy like Plato, yet he preferred aristocracy to a democratic government. He even contended under certain conditions, the judgment of a few could be equal to or wiser than that of the will of many. According to Aristotle, the upper class contained people of the greater refinement or quality and as such they were best equipped to provide better government for the society as a whole {Baradat 2000:67}

SELF-ASSESSMENT EXERCISE 2

Analyse the differences between monarchy and aristocracy.

3.3   Theocracy

Theocracy is a government by divine guidance or by officials who are regarded as divinely guided. Theocracy means literally 'the rule of God' and the term was invented by Josephus (AD 38-*c.* 100), to describe the ancient Hebrew constitution and the role of Mosaic Law. Theocracy can also be defined as a government by a priesthood or religious leader. It is divine and the laws made are of divine inspiration. In many theocracies, government's leaders are members of the clergy or Islamic clerics, and the state's legal system is based on religious laws. Theocratic rule was typical of early civilizations. However, the era of Enlightenment marked the end of theocracy. The Vatican City in Rome, for example, is a theocratic state headed by the Pope. Other contemporary examples of countries practicing theocracy include Saudi Arabia and Iran. A more secular version of the meaning of theocracy is that it is priestly rule.

In theocracies, the religiously revealed laws or policies are unchallengeable, even by a popular majority or by an inherited monarch. It should however be noted that even such regimes which claim that their laws are divinely ordained and thus immutable, do not make this claim in respect of all laws. Theocracy is a form of government in which a god or deity is recognized as the state's supreme civil ruler, or in a higher sense, a form of government in which a state is governed by immediate divine guidance or by officials who are regarded as divinely guided.

For believers, theocracy is a form of government in which divine power governs an earthly human state, either in a personal incarnation or, more often, via religious institutional representatives such as the church, replacing or dominating civil government. Theocracy should be distinguished from other secular forms of government that have a state religion, or are merely influenced by theological or moral concepts, and monarchies , which is based on divine rights of king. A theocracy may be monist in form, where the administrative hierarchy of the government is identical with the administrative hierarchy of the religion, or it may be dualist, having two arms, in which the state's administrative hierarchy is subordinate to the religious hierarchy. Theocracy is also a form of government where people do not govern; it is God who governs through the priests. By not separating religion from the state, Islam also sanctions theocracy.

SELF-ASSESSMENT EXERCISE 3

Differentiate theocratic from a secular government.

3.4   Totalitarianism/Dictatorship

Since the 1950s, some scholars have argued that the extreme type of authoritarianism is best described as "totalitarianism." Robert C. Fried (1966:3) noted that totalitarian and dictatorial institutions related, but they differ in one respect. The characteristics of the former include complete control over government, complete autonomy from outside and total control of social life. The latter shares the first two characteristics of the former, but does not possess control over social life. The nature of government of government is important, since it determines the burden the political leadership shoulders. If a government is dictatorial, the burden is heavy. This is unlike a democracy where the burden does not disappear but the people share it.

In addition to the characteristics already cited above, "totalitarianism" implies "an official ideology which members of the society must adhere to and which covers all aspects of life in the society"; "a system of terroristic police control which supports, and supervises on behalf of the leader, and which is directed against the 'enemies' of the State"; and "central control and direction of the entire economy." Other characteristics of totalitarianism include the subordination of all to the interest of the political elites and to the specification of the ideology designed and adopted by them. In a totalitarian state, all groups the youth, labor unions, cultural associations and other intermediate social structures including the educational system are organized to serve the interest of the state and its rulers.

Indeed, there is no distinction between the state and society. While the ruler controls sophisticated state apparatus of propaganda to communicate and force the will of the political leadership on the citizens, there are no institutional channels for assuring feed back communication from the population to the elites. In short, authoritarian governments are content to control the overt behaviour of the citizen and to eliminate any sign of organized opposition. Totalitarian governments attempt to control not only their citizen behaviour but their thoughts as well. So instead of the dictators giving the people cutleries to make them survive, they throw cutlasses at them to make them fight the war to defend their rulers.

But ironically, history is replete with major achievements recorded by some dictatorial leaders: In spite of the notorious Nazi concentration camps Hitler rebuilt a shattered German economy and conceptualized a Volkswagen, a "people's car"; while Stalin's desperate struggle to even out with the United States at the onset of the cold war did not stop him from transforming the Soviet Union from a backward agrarian to a military superpower. Chairman Mao also put China out of a primitive state, and transformed it into an atomic power (Anyanwu 2002:209).

SELF-ASSESSMENT EXERCISE 4

Explain the distinguishing features of a democracy and totalitarianism

4.0   SUMMARY

We have examined in this unit different forms of governments. We first discussed the monarchy as a hereditary institution headed by a person, who rules either as an absolute ruler, or in other circumstances, as a constitutional monarch. We also examined aristocracy, which is a form of government headed by men of rare attributes of virtue, distinction and valor. We also treated theocracy as a form of government in which the state makes no distinction between the divine/ spiritual and temporal or secular. We finally discussed a totalitarian government as the type in which fundamental human rights of the citizens are suppressed, and where no distinction is made between the state and society.

5.0   CONCLUSION

Each of these forms of government at different times in the development of political institutions occupied a central place in the running of human society. While monarchy is obviously the first and earliest known form of government, and its prominence as a form of government can be dated to the pre-Enlightenment epoch when it was sustained by the divine right of the King. Both aristocracy and theocracy also competed with monarchy, but the latter seems to have survived the challenge, since only few countries subscribed to either aristocracy or theocracy. Irrespective of its form, a government has to fulfill certain basic tasks. It has to keep the nation alive, guard its independence and preserve its cohesion.

6.0   TUTOR-MARKED ASSIGNMENTS

1.   Describe the major characteristics of the Monarchy in Britain.
2.   Examine the features of the government in The Vatican, which makes it a Theocracy.
3.   Critically analyse the system of government in Saudi Arabia to examine the characteristics of a Monarchy or Theocracy.

UNIT 7   DEMOCRACY AS A FORM OF GOVERNMENT

1.0   Introduction
2.0   Objectives
3.0   Main Contents
    3.1   The Meaning and Features of Democracy
    3.2   The Process of Democracy
    3.3   The Criticisms and Limitations of Democracy
4.0   Summary
5.0   Conclusion
6.0   Tutor-Marked Assignments

1.0   INTRODUCTION

Democracy is one form, perhaps the most popular and controversial type of government. It had its origin in the Greek- city states, but it has become an acceptable form of government in other parts of the world, and has been adapted by many societies to suit their different peculiarities. This unit examines the meaning and principles of democracy as a philosophical and political concept.

It also discusses the established process of democracy, otherwise called Western liberal democracy through which nations seek to realize the goal of a democratic system.

2.0   OBJECTIVES

At the end of this unit, you should be able to:

- explain in details, features of democracy as a system of government
- discuss how a state can realize the goals of a democratic government
- analyse why democracy is not a perfect form of government from its theoretical and practical perspectives.

3.0   MAIN CONTENT

3.1   The Meaning and Features of Democracy

The term democracy comes from the Greek word for "rule of the people." The Greek's idea of democracy was based on the full participation of all people in every aspect of government. The Greek system of democratic government is the model of "pure" or consensus" democracy, though in the case of Greek pure democracy did not last long. However, the idea of government by the people survived the decline of the Greek city-state to become one of the basic ideals of political thought. There are two broad categories of scholars on the concept of democracy: the process and principle democrats. Process scholars see democracy as a way of making decisions, but principle democrats' argue that democracy has a very important theoretical base (Baradat, 2000). The principle democrats' states that, although the procedure of democracy is important, according to them it is secondary to the basic intents and objectives of democracy as expressed in democratic theory. For this reason, we will focus in this unit on the principle or theory of democracy.

The principle democrats contend that the basic principle of modern liberal democracy include that the individual is of major importance in the society, that each individual is basically equal to all other individuals, and that each has certain inalienable rights. Central to democracy is also the assumption of the freedom of choice that the individual has from form fear or coercion and any other disabilities. Central to democracy is liberty to make choice and equality of choice. Democracy, according to John Dewey is much more than a form of government or a set of legal arrangement, but should be seen as a way of life that requires faith in the capacity of human beings for intelligent judgment and action, if proper conditions are provided. He argues further that democracy requires faith in the possibility of resolving disputes through un- coerced deliberations. Democracy, according to Dewey, should not be viewed as "something institutional and external" but should been seen as "a way of personal life."

Democracy not only requires institutional guarantees of rights but also faith in the possibility of resolving disputes through un-coerced deliberation. In other words, un-hindered communication should be put in place in a democratic setting in which there is a "cooperative undertaking", instead of having one group suppress the other through either subtle or overt violence or through intimidation. Democracy does not impose authority from above but instead relies on the dialogue as the source of authority and the means of choosing among competing alternatives. A democratic system flourishes in a setting where there is unlimited participation of all citizens in a free and rational public debate.

For Emile Durkheim, the basic hallmark of democracy is the citizens' capacity to participate in the state's judgment. To him, the state's legitimacy springs from its collective conscience. In other words, the citizens should be able to contribute to the natural reasoning and deliberations of the society. In Durkheim's view, if we want to have a viable democracy then we must have a vibrant public sphere where issues of common concern could be debated in a rational manner. Similarly, intolerance, abuse, calling of names because of differences of opinion about religion or politics including differences of race, colour or wealth are treason to the democratic way of life.

Despite this seeming agreement by most scholars on its principle, democracy, especially its process, which we shall discuss in the next unit, is, essentially, a largely contested concept. Robert Dahl (1984) sees it as a concept that defies definition in the sense that the way one defines it would betray one's beliefs, personal outlook, political experience and ideological preference. There are differences for example between the United States' and the Soviet Union's conception of democracy. A major difference between USA and the former Soviet Union is that US emphasizes political freedom as basic to democracy while USSR focuses on economic rights and its leaders are even prepared to suppress or deny individual rights for the sake of the survival of the system. On the other hand, democracy in the USA does not place high premium on economic needs, in spite of President Franklin Delano Roosevelt's New Deal program. In retrospect, one can argue that that one of the reasons why the Soviet Union collapsed is that the system could no longer fulfill the basic economic needs of its people despite the lid the system placed on human (political) rights. This is why Baradat (2000:66) argued that the Soviet Union and the United States differed as to which procedures best defines democracy".

SELF-ASSESSMENT EXERCISE 1

Define the concept of Democracy and outline its main features

3.2   The process of democracy

The popular definition of democracy offered by Abraham Lincoln gives the impression that all the citizens have the opportunities of participating in government. However, this is no longer possible in the modern world because of the size of sovereign states today. Since the world has advanced beyond the Greek city-states participatory democracy is no longer practicable, hence the necessity for indirect or representative democracy. Through this process, given that all necessary conditions are in place, it is quite possible to achieve the ideals of democracy. Political power comes from the people and that a government is only legally constituted and run when the people gives their consent. The democratic process is therefore the institutional arrangements for arriving at political decisions in which individual acquires and retain the power to rule by means of a competitive struggle for the people's vote.

The success of any democratic political system is largely, determined by the willingness on the part of the political actors to comply with the rules of the game. A democratic political system will therefore be stable if the process of leadership recruitment is legitimate and majority of the citizens accept the electoral system as fair and just. Presently, the United States and most European countries have succeeded in meeting most conditions for the sustenance of democracy, while most third world countries are still struggling to lay the foundation or rudiments, in order to begin the democratic journey. Democracy goes beyond mere putting in place political structures and institutions, but also involves meaningful participation of the peoples in the affairs of the state. The key words therefore are participation, transparency and accountability.

As aptly argued by Samuel P. Huntington (Huntington, 1991), democracy has advanced in waves since the early nineteenth Century, with each wave giving way to partial reversals followed by new gains. The current wave, which is the third one, according to him, commenced in the mid-seventies. Thus, contemporary views on democracy see it as the exercise of state power with the consent of the people either directly or indirectly through their elected representatives. Within democratic governance there is provision for state institutions to express the will of the state and ultimately for the supremacy of that expression on all basic questions of socioeconomic direction and policy. Under democratic governance, factors such as economic equality, fraternal feeling and political liberty within a defined territory are indispensable pre-requisites.

The institutional expression within democratic governance in contemporary times are equal rights for all normal adults to vote and to stand as candidates for election; periodic elections; equal eligibility for executive and judicial offices (provided the essential qualifications for the performance of the assigned duties are satisfied) and freedom of speech, publication and association (Appadoria, 2004:137). These rights in themselves provide opportunities for the entire citizenry to participate in choosing their rulers and in deciding the general lines of their policy via their political manifestos presented before elections. However, a number of factors, most significant of which are the social environment, economic resource of the citizens and their natural endowment decide the extent to which these essential democratic *sine qua non* rights can be met.

Nonetheless, in most democratic states in spite of their imperfections, even the poor are given minimal equality of voting during elections since votes are counted, not weighed, regardless of the social or economic status of the voters. Among such rights that can promote the cause of democracy are freedoms of speech, press and association.

These rights are integral to democratic governance because they make possible free discussion and the continuous participation of the citizenry in government, overtime and not only during the time of general elections. Free discussion is necessary because democratic governance is based on the belief in the value of individual personality. This implies the obligation to respect the other man, to listen to his views and to take into account his point of argument. In addition, the process of law making should allow full scope for the consideration of different and opposing viewpoints. Those who are inevitably affected by a law must be content that their case has been properly heard in a properly constituted court of law in the land (Egbewole; 2008: 214-5).

This makes the 'Rule of Law' a cardinal element of democracy (Dicey 1963). Equality before the law, impartiality in the dispensation of justice and periodic elections are also important in promoting hitch-free democratic process. There is also the possibility of an alternative government in democratic governance. This is in sharp contrast to a situation where power is conferred permanently, or where people do not feel free or safe to discuss or vote according to the dictates of their conscience. Where this is the case then democracy cannot be said to exist even if the people continue to enjoy the other political rights enumerated above.

Finally, democratic governance requires proper organization and dynamic leadership. Political parties carry out organization within democratic governance. Despite their limitations or weaknesses, political parties are indispensable to the successful operation of a democratic society (Bello-imam, 2002:14-16). Little wonder political parties are regarded as the fulcrum of democracy. Lastly, we must point out that it is not possible to isolate the principle of democracy from its process because one needs to reconcile the two in such a way that a state should use the right method or process to achieve the objectives of democracy.

SELF-ASSESSMENT EXERCISE 2

Explain how the process of democracy helps to realize its underlying principles.

3.3   Criticisms and Limitations of Democracy

Democracy as a philosophical and political process has been subjected to a number criticisms. Joseph Schumpeter for example argued that liberty and equality are not part of democracy and that in all democratic systems; there are necessarily limitations with respect to the qualifications and circumstances of voters. The franchise is often qualified and the qualifications exclude significant section of the population from the voting process. As for equality, the scholar argued that the relationship between the voter and the candidate is that people who are slightly affluent in the society are more able to make claims or enjoy democratic dividends. Besides, disparities in educational, economic or other social conditions limit the real opportunities for the voters to exercise their franchise in spite of apparent equality.

Another criticism of democracy derives from elite theories best associated with Mosca and Pareto. According to these theorists, in most societies, past and present, there is the distinction between the ruler and the ruled. Indeed, the Platonic idea of philosopher king is considered a tacit legitimization of elitist rule. The processes and conditions of governance also have their own internal dynamics and logic, which gradually create a distinction in outlook and opportunities between those who govern and those who are governed. Both Michel Aaron J. J. Rousseau had argued that democracy necessarily involves representation in which some interest may not receive adequate attention of the elected representatives. Harold Laski (1982:319) shares this sentiment when he advised that an elected representative is "not entitled to get elected as a free trader and to vote (in Parliament) for a protective tariff".

By virtue of their positions, the representatives possess greater political power than the average citizens do. This is because they meet and operate on a regular basis and are better informed about the technicalities of the law and of socio-political relationsthan the larger society they represent. Although the majority has the power of ejection and rejection, the power is exercised irregularly, i.e. at long intervals during elections. Consequently, Michel Aaron argued that government by the people is an illusion since the great majority of people are uneducated or uninformed and therefore cannot participate effectively, or at all, in the process of government. Democracy is also attacked as slow and inefficient. The mechanism for decision-making is long and tortuous, unable to make speedy decision in an emergency. While democracy might have been possible in the past, technology has complicated society to such an extent that popular government is no longer possible.

In developing societies, according to Lucien Pye, democracy has also been criticized for being inefficient: "To a disturbing degree the strange idea has been spread within many transitional societies that democracy is linked with inefficiency, muddled actions and corrupt practices while authoritarian ways are identified with clear thinking, purposeful action and firm dedication." This essentially constituted the rationale put forward by African leaders in the first decade of independence for their preference, for one party democracy, which in reality was a euphemism for dictatorship. Finally, democracy is also fraught with the problem of illogicality because it tends to promote mediocrity at the expense of merit. In political contests, winners are not always the best candidate in terms of intellect, education or competency. Rather, the criteria for determining electoral victory are popularity, financial wherewithal and other factors.

Nevertheless, democracy is still the most popular and rational form of government. According to Obafemi Awolowo (1981), "There is indeed no substitute to democracy as a form of government. It is most certainly the best form of government, which mankind in its long, painful and heroic search, has evolved." Democracy is so popular that most countries, even those that are clearly undemocratic like the Peoples Democratic Republic in Korea, or China, or the former German Democratic Republic (GDR) prefer to preface their names or pretend to practice democracy. However, in reality, these are states which operate authoritarian form of government, and are/or one party based, a factor which explains the potential for authoritarianism in such states.

In the Western liberal tradition of Europe and North America, and those areas of the world that emulate them, the tendency is towards multi-party democracy. The preference for the multi party system is because it allows for competition between parties, sometimes of different ideological persuasions, with an inherent likelihood of transfer of power from one party to another, in accordance with the wishes of the electoral majority, if the ruling party is defeated. For the less developed countries, a lot still need to be done to institute the practice of democracy. As the Jacobins of France once said, "The transition of an oppressed people to democracy is like the effort by which nature arose from nothingness to existence"

SELF-ASSESSMENT EXERCISE 3

Discuss the major criticisms and limitations of democracy?

4.0   SUMMARY

We have discussed in this unit the origins, meaning and features of democracy. We observed that democracy in its classical conception has intrinsic value, yet we recognized that in the modern world of large nation-states it is no longer practicable to have the benefits of direct democracy. The idea of representative government has therefore become the only way by which political leadership can be recruited on a regular basis, and they will retain their positions as long as they continue to enjoy the support of the people. However, we also noted that the process of enthroning a democratic government may not be perfect. Consequently, the reality today is that democracy as a form of government has been subjected to a lot of abuses, principal of which is the substitution of elite or minority for majority rule, in many countries.

5.0   CONCLUSION

Democracy has often been described as the best form of government. One major reason for the popularity of democracy as a form of government is that it rests on the consent of the people. Invariably, it is popular support that makes a government laying claims to democratic values to earn legitimacy. Democracy is also seen as form of government that maximizes participation; promotes accountability in government and make conditions for the realization of social justice possible. But for most societies especially in the developing world, democracy is a journey or dream, not a destination since there is no perfect democracy anywhere in the world. Indeed, there is no country in the world today in which the political system approximates what is known as the classical conception of democratic principle.

6.0   TUTOR-MARKED ASSIGNMENTS

1.   explain the difference between Democracy and Dictatorship.
2.   give reasons why democracy is no longer practicable in its classical and direct form in the modern world.
3.   discuss features of a political system that promotes the attainment of the principles and objectives of a democratic order.

MODULE 3   POLITICAL/PARTY SYSTEMS AND ELECTORAL SYSTEMS

UNIT 1   MAJOR COMPONENTS OF A POLITICAL SYSTEM

1.0   Introduction
2.0   Objectives
3.0   Main Contents
      3.1   Political institutions
      3.2   Elites
      3.3   Masses
      3.4   Political Culture
      3.5   Political Linkage
4.0   Summary
5.0   Conclusion
6.0   Tutor- Marked Assignments

1.0 INTRODUCTION

In any political system, there are basic components that must work in a state of harmony before the system can be said to be stable or in a state of equilibrium. It is also possible disaggregate a political system into its components with a view to knowing which of the components is malfunctioning, which may contribute to system breakdown, failure or collapse. In this Unit we shall look at the various components of a political system and how they interact and are related to one another contributing

2.0   OBJECTIVES

At the end of this unit, you should be able to:

- articulate the meaning and relevance of each components of a political system
- discuss the relationship between each of the components and their impacts on the political system
- explain the optimal functionality of a political system given a properly integrated component parts with interdependence as well as their respective equilibrium.

3.0   MAIN CONTENT

A checklist of the main elements and themes most commonly studied in any political system, and which are relevant in politics and the political process include political institutions, elites, masses and political culture.

3.1   Political Institutions

Perhaps the most important and visible foundations of the political system or process are the formal institutions of government such as: the Constitutions, Parliaments, Court, Bureaucracies, and Executive structure. These political institutions serve as the focal points for deciding, "Who get what, when and how." They also serve as the arena of the political process, the structure of a nation's political system undoubtedly influence and shapes its policy-making processes. The questions could be asked: to what extent can the political stability in USA and Britain be attributed to the specific structure of their political institutions? Could the political instability that besets third world counties be remedied by changing their political system to make them more like that of the Americans or English? Providing answers to these questions was a major challenge and pre-occupation of Political Scientists, until the advent of the Behavioral Revolution.

One of the most significant contributions of the Behavioral Revolution to the development of political science is to stress the importance of the human element over and above institutions, systems, and structure and the realization that they cannot be understood in isolation. They can only be meaningful, and be better appreciated within the context of the operators, and cannot work if the human behavioral element is not conducive to the systemic or institutional requirements. In other words, no political structure can endure in the absence of corresponding values. The character of Nigerian politics in the First Republic when the parliamentary system was used, and the second when the presidential model was adopted as a possible, better alternative goes to show that explanations for the success and failure of political systems are located beyond a system or its structure.

SELF-ASSESSMENT EXERCISE 1

Assess the importance of political institutions in a political system.

3.2   Political Elites

The formal structures of the government are central in explaining the three basic questions posed by Harold Lasswell: "who get what, when and how? However, the study and the understanding of the primacy of the elites are more important in analyzing the relationships among the other components, especially the masses. Elites dominate formal institutions of government, they get most of what is available to be shared or allocated authoritatively. Indeed, a significant school of political scientists suggests that elites, defined as decision makers, are perhaps the single most important elements in the political process. In their view, the American and British political systems are stable because of high level of consensus among the elites as to the rules of the game. The dominant elites always stick together; they are conscious of their enlightened self-interest and know how to use their privileged positions, in addition to the dominated or weakened status of the masses to advance these interests. On the other hand, the chaos and the mounting violence in the politics of third world countries can also be attributed to the lack of consensus among competing political elites.

3.2.1 Elite theory

Geraint Parry in his *Political Elites* stress that elites are the "decision makers of the society whose power is not subject to control by any other body in the society". He then defined Elite as the small minority who appear to play an exceptionally influential part in political and social affairs of that group which appears to wield control over crucial policies. In political science, elite theory is class approach to the understanding of political process. The elite can be divided into governed elite and non-governed elite. The assumptions underlying the elite theory are:

- That in every society there is always a minority of the population which takes major decisions. Such decisions are usually referred to as political decisions
- That elites include those who occupy political power or seek to influence government decisions

- That there is circulation of elites

That there are no changes in society about the composition or structure of the elites Robert Michell in 1942 formulated the famous "Iron Law of Oligarchy": "He who says organization says Oligarchy". According to the elite theorists, "government by the people for the people" is a farce. On their part, the ruling elites always self-righteously argue that they are not anti-masses, but they as the leaders of their various factions have the right to determine the orientation of policy to be pursued by the government in power.

SELF-ASSESSMENT EXERCISE 2

Analyse the relevance of elite theory to mass participation in politics.

3.3   The Masses

The Microsoft Encarta dictionary 2008 defines the word *masses* (a plural form of mass) as a body of matter that forms a whole but has no definable shape. Therefore, the downtrodden, ordinary citizens (known as the average person) who are pliable to manipulations by the elites in the society could be defined as the masses. Unlike the formal institutions or the Elites, the influence of the masses upon policy is usually indirect and difficult to measure. Rather than the movers and shakers of society, the masses tend to be the moved and the shaken. The masses do influence policy, because it is the masses that the elites must control if they are to remain in power and it is the masses that must be mobilized if the elites are to achieve their goals. As an illustration, although elites make the formal decision on whether to declare wars, it is the masses that fight wars. The motivation` and skill of the masses do make a difference in the outcome of war. Indeed, the profound willingness of the masses in advanced countries to play by the rules and support their respective systems offers at least a partial explanation for their stability. The reverse is also true for African states.

How readily the masses can be mobilized to support elite goals, then, depends, in large measure upon their perception and evaluation of the political system. The more that the masses are deeply committed to the political system, the more stable a regime is likely to be. The less committed the masses, the less stable the political system is likely to be. The overall assessment of the manner in which the masses perceive and evaluate the political system is often referred to as political culture. The process by which individuals learn or otherwise acquire their political culture is often referred to as process of political socialization.

SELF-ASSESSMENT EXERCISE 3

Explain why the impact of the masses in the political process is disproportionate to their number.

3.4   Political Culture

A political culture according to Allan Ball (1979:56) is composed of the attitudes, beliefs emotions and values of society that relates to the political system and to political issues. In short, it is the study of a people's orientation to politics or what people think about it, as distinct from the actual political behaviour. Two components are critical in understanding political culture: the attitude to the political institutions of the state, and the degree to which citizens feel they can influence and participate in the decision making process. The latter is otherwise called the degree or level of political efficacy. In liberal democracies, political culture is transmitted from one generation to another, through established societal institutions. This is achieved through the process of political socialization.

What is relevant to a democratic system is what has been called "the civic culture" which is most likely to ensure political stability. In a parochial political culture, citizens are dimly aware of the existence of a central government. In a subject political culture, citizens see themselves as subjects of a government, and not a participant, while in the participant political culture citizens are keenly involved in political activities, contribute to it, and are affected by it.

SELF-ASSESSMENT EXERCISE 4

Discuss the relevance of political culture to the problem of political instability.

3.5   Political Linkage

The ability of the elites to control and mobilize the masses, including their ability to socialize the masses to believe in the political system, depends in large measure upon the elites who dominate those instructions. The more that the political system penetrates the masses, the more readily the elite can communicate its wishes and coordinate the mobilization of the masses in fulfillment of these wishes.

The more that the political system can penetrate the masses, the more readily the elite can assess mass demand and either take steps to meet them: thereby building supports for the system, or take defensive action. The more that the political system penetrates the masses, the more difficult it is for opposition to the system to develop un-noticed by the dominant elite. The linkage mechanisms that link the masses and elites include political parties, pressure groups such as labor unions and professional organizations. In less developed societies, the linkage process often relies on kinship and religious networks. Through public opinion, the citizens of a country can also influence the conduct of government officials. It is a popular axiom that the glory of the king or government must find its expression in the welfare of the people.

SELF-ASSESSMENT EXERCISE 5

Explain how developed the linkage mechanisms or devises in your country are.

4.0   SUMMARY

In this unit, we have examined the major components of a political system. We identified the elites, who in spite of their limited number occupy a dominant position in any political system. We also explained that, on the other hand, the masses do not enjoy a decisive influence that is commensurate to their numerical strength. We further noted that for a political system to remain stable and endure the linkage mechanisms that bind the masses to the system must be strong enough to make the political system fulfill its goals, as determined by the elites, and without resistance from the masses.

5.0   CONCLUSION

Political Systems tends to reflect the interests of those who have created them, and in most instances, it is the powerful actors within a society that creates its political institutions. The stability of every political system depends on how the different components seamlessly fit together in a manner that the system performs the four main functions of goal attainment, pattern maintenance, adaptation and integration. Also important, for any political system to perform optimally and avoid system decline, decay or break-down, it must in addition enjoy the interdependence and equilibrium of its different parts or components.

6.0   TUTOR-MARKED ASSIGNMENT

1.   Explain the roles played by the linkage mechanisms in a political system.
2.   Discuss why the impact of the masses in a political system is disproportionate to their number
3.   Analyse the roles played by the linkage mechanisms in a political system.

UNIT 2 THE MEANING AND NATURE OF POLITICAL PARTIES

1.0   INTRODUCTION

In this unit, you will be introduced to political parties, the definitions given to them by scholars as well their classifications by using their number, among other criteria, as a basis or the most popular criterion for this classification. We will also discuss the structure and organization of party system with a view to bringing out the differences between parties in the developed and developing countries. In a separate section, we will examine the role of political parties as a vehicle for representative government by looking at the functions they perform.

2.0   OBJECTIVES

At the end of this unit, you should be able to:

*   define political parties and classify them into different types.
*   explain the   structures
        organization and operations of party systems
*   discuss the functions they perform and why they are
        indispensable in a democracy.

3.0   MAIN CONTENT

3.1   Definition and origins of political parties

Scholars and political philosophers have defined political parties in several ways. Edmund Burke defined a political party as "a body of men united for promoting by their joint endeavors the national interest upon some political principle in which they are agreed." In Joseph Schesinger's conceptualization, parties are political organizations, which actively and effectively engage in a competition for elective office. According to Joseph LaPalombara (1974:323), a political party is "a formal organization whose self-conscious, primary purpose is to place and maintain in public office persons who will control alone or in coalition, the machinery of government". In the view of Joseph Schumpeter (1943:279) "The first and foremost aim of each political party is to prevail over the others in order to get into power or to say in it" Thus, Political parties, like interest groups are organizations seeking influence over government; they can be distinguished from interest groups on the basis of their primary political orientation.

Political parties developed along with the expansion of suffrage-the right to vote-and can be understood only in the context of elections. In Nigeria for example, the first political party in the country was the National Democratic Party (NNDP) that was formed by Hebert Macaulay in 1922 to contest the Lagos Town Council election created when the elective principle was introduced under the Clifford Constitution. A party seeks to control the entire government by electing its members to office thereby controlling the government personnel. Interest groups through campaign contributions and other forms of electoral assistance are also interested in getting politicians-especially those who are inclined in their policy direction elected. But interest groups are not interested in directly sponsoring candidates for elections, and in between elections they usually accept government and its personnel as given and try to influence government policies through them. While interest groups are benefit seekers, political parties are office-seekers.

In an elaborate and expansive definition, Leslie Lipson (1964:120) defines a political party thus:

Whenever sufficient diversity of interests occurs among those who compose a society and the political system gives these interests an opportunity to combine, men will cluster into groupings, which may be more or less formal, and closely or loosely organized. They do this in order better to protect what they may possess and extend their influence to wider spheres.

In simple language, a political party is a group of persons bonded in policy and opinion in support of a general political cause, which essentially is the pursuit, and retention for as long as democratically feasible, of government and its offices. In other words, a political party is a group that seeks to elect candidates to public offices by supplying them with a label - a party identification - by which they are known to the electorate. Therefore, a political party is composed of a group of people like any other groups or organizations, except that it is distinguished by its unique objective, which, in a democratic setting, is seeking control of government through nominating its candidates and presenting programs for endorsement via the electoral process in competition with other parties.

SELF-ASSESSMENT EXERCISE 1

Describe in your own words a political party.

3.2   Organization and Structure of Party Systems

Party organization is the internal arrangement by which parties are structured in such a way that it is better able to fulfill its mission. It is possible that we may have one or few parties that know their limitations, and may not pretend to cover the whole country; but most parties prefer to have presence in every part of a country. The advantage of this is that the more widespread the party support base is, the better the prospects of it winning an election, if the right conditions are in place.

Indeed, in Nigeria since 1979, until the liberalization of conditions for the operations of political parties under the Obasanjo's civilian administration, political parties were required to have membership and offices in at least two thirds of the states in the federation, before they could qualify for registration.

In most countries, parties are organized in such a way that they have branches at every tier or level of government: National, State and Local levels. In addition, taken a cue from the United States, Nigeria since the Babangida's transition program, has promoted the grassroots politics by making the ward level the centrepiece of political activities through to the national level of party organization. The ward level is so important today that a presidential aspirant may have his national ambition truncated, no matter how popular he may be elsewhere, if he is unable to be selected as a delegate from his own ward. This is why most aspirants for political offices are always interested in having their men constituting the majority in the party executives at all levels.

Beyond the party's official executive organs, there are other levels of party organization. These include the Central Working Committee (CWC), Board of Trustees (BOT), the Elders' Council, the Parliamentary or Legislative Caucus, the Party's Governors' Forum, the Women and Youth Wing. Experience has shown that in most states, including advanced democracies, only aspirants who can get the nod from these unofficial levels can hope to become a party's candidate or flag-bearers during general elections. In Nigeria, for example, given the electoral dominance that the Peoples Democratic

Party (PDP) has enjoyed in the last ten years, the competition within the party has always been the keenest in the country. This is because of the plausible assumption by most aspirants that whoever becomes the party's candidate is almost certain of winning the elections in most states, including the presidency.

In recent times, the Governors Forum, or more appropriately, PDP Governors' Forum has proved to be the most decisive platform of taking crucial decisions, for the party, and indeed, for the nation as shown in the elevation of Jonathan Goodluck as Nigeria's Acting President. The implication of the new found powers of these unofficial organs of political parties is that party's primaries and conventions have been turn into a mere ritual only to decorate those that have been anointed by the dominant groups within the party.

SELF-ASSESSMENT EXERCISE 2

Compare a party's structure and organization in a developed with that of a developing country.

3.3   Types of Party System

A party system is a network of relationships through which parties interact and influence the political process. The most popular way of distinguishing between different types of party system is the reference to the number of parties competing for power. The French political scientist, Maurice Durverger in his popular work *Political Parties* classified parties in to three types: The single or one party system, the two party systems and the multiple party systems.

3.3.1 Single or one-party system

A one party is a system in which only one party is legal recognized in the country. Therefore, it is illegal for any organization to operate as a political party in such country. It is a common feature of communist and socialist countries like North Korea, Cuba etc. In the immediate post independent period, one party was a feature of scores of African countries such as Ghana under Kwame Nkrumah where the Convention Peoples Party (CPP) held sway and Tanzania under Julius Nyerere where the Tanzanian African National Union (TANU) was the only officially recognized party. The position of the PDP as the party controlling the federal government in Nigeria does not make the country a one party state; it only represents a case of one party dominant regime.

You should note the following as important characteristics of a one party state: no opposition party is legally recognized, there is usually only one ideology for the whole country, and it is the ideology of the party in government. There is also either no private control of mass media or very stringent requirements before private individuals can be allowed to own or publish a newspaper or magazine, in addition to close censorship of their activities. Those who promote one party system advance the following advantages:

- One party prevents economic waste in the sense that elections are not held among numerous parties most of which are not viable or strong enough to win a single seat. The resources to provide logistics and security during elections are channel to other uses.
- One party also promotes unity since the only recognized party must of necessity cuts across ethnic or religious divides in a country it therefore has the advantage of promoting national unity.
- It ensures stability in the sense that there is no opposition party that may overheat the polity through acrimonious competitions for power during elections. Unhealthy rivalry for political power may evoke unpatriotic sentiments by bad losers.
- In a one-party system, decision-making process is prompt since the dilatory tactics of the opposition parties in government or filibustering of opposition members in parliament are avoided.
- There is also absence of political vendetta against political opponents. Good as one-party system appears to be, one of its greatest drawbacks is that it may develop into a dictatorship.

Other disadvantages to note include: Individual rights are usually trampled upon. This is common in most one-party system whether in developed or developing societies. The human rights abuse under Joseph Stalin era in the former Soviet Union, the 1989 massacre at the Tiananmen Square in China and the Kwame Nkrumah's Preventive Detention Act are vivid examples. The implication of this is that the principle of rule of law and provisions of the constitution on fundamental human rights may not be followed or guaranteed.

The constitution may be silent on the need for periodic elections, and where such provisions are made, elections are only held to confirm the same party in power, or a mere ritual for public relation exercise.

3.3.2 Two party systems

A two party system operates in a country where only two parties have reasonable chances of winning elections, forming or controlling the government. This does not however suggest that only two parties exist in a country. But among the multitude of parties that participate in the electoral process only two of them are strong enough to win elections. In the United States and Great Britain, where two party systems operates, the two parties, the Democratic and Republican Parties in the former, and the Conservative and the Labor Parties in the latter, are products of historical evolution. The Nigerian example when President Babangida decreed into existence the Social Democratic Party and the Republican Convention during the Nigeria's ill-fated Third Republic was a clear aberration.

In U.S.A. and Britain, the two parties have been alternating, sometimes in succession, in forming the governments in their countries. In Britain, for example, during the World War II era, the Conservative Party was the ruling party, but Winston Churchill's gallantry, as a wartime political leader did not stop the British voters from voting in Clement Atlee in 1945. This led to the saying "The electors cheered Churchill but voted against him." But in the United States the American rewarded the Commander of the Allied Forces during the same war, Dwight Eisenhower of the Republican Party with victory in spite of the fact that Franklin Delano Roosevelt took U S to the war, and Harry Truman also of the Democratic Party won the war, which stamped American leadership of the world.

The greatest advantage of two party systems is that it promotes political stability by providing for the possibility of alternative governments. There is also room and opportunity for choice of candidates and parties' manifestos. It is democratic because it accommodates democratic principle and allows the operation of rule of law. Regular alternation or change of government is possible because there is the provision for periodic elections. This gives the electorates the power to change a government that is not responsive or accountable.

Two party-systems also provides for stronger opposition, which makes for a better government since the ruling party is always cautious of the policies it is pursuing. The opposition is therefore seen as a corrective party government; since it watches over and offer criticisms of the ruling party. This promotes stability unlike in a multi-party system where multiplicity of parties encourages proliferation of, sometimes conflicting, ideas, and formation of coalition governments. From the experience of both matured and developing societies such coalition arrangements usually an alliance of strange bedfellows, more often than not, produce weak and unstable governments.

The following are the disadvantages of a two party system. There is the danger that the two party systems may divide the country into two opposing factions. This can polarize a country along religious and ethnic divides, and may thereby negatively affect or endanger national unity. It may also lead to one party state if one of two parties retains power for a disproportionately long period; this may tempt the other parties to dissolve into the ruling party

3.3.3 Multi party system

A multi party system exists in a country where there are several parties, and there is the possibility that each of them has reasonable chance of winning seats in the legislature. This model is suitable in a country where there is multiplicity of, sometimes minority, interests in which case each of these parties will represent such interests. Germany offers a good example of a multi-party system where the parties in the country represent diverse interests such as religion, gender and environmental. Nigeria is also a good example of a multi-party system with parties such as the Action Congress (AC), All Nigerian Peoples Party (ANPP), and Labor Party (LP) etc struggling to wrestle power at the centre from the Peoples Democratic Party (PDP) that has been in power at the federal level since 1999.

Multi party system can also be defined as a system with more than two political parties are contesting for political power in a country. All the parties are duly registered and recognized by law. Nigeria in the Second Republic with six political parties: NPN UPN NPP GNPP PRP and NAP Babarinsa (2003), and Fourth Republic with about fifty parties is a multi party state. Other countries in the same group include France, Italy and Germany. In a multi-party system a coalition government may be formed among political parties with reasonable number of seats in parliament.

The greatest advantage of multi-party systems is that individuals can easily make free choice of parties and program. There is also absence of dictatorship, due to multiplicity of parties that are always ready to put the leadership of the ruling party on its toes. Fundamental human rights of the citizens are also better guaranteed and protected by the government, which also make for wider representation of peoples of different interests and opinion in the decision making process. Multi party system also presents its own drawbacks. They include the following: Too many political programs are offered to the voters, which may confuse them and make electoral choice difficult to make; it is also very expensive to manage because of the huge costs involved in party organization, voters' mobilization and campaigns as well as the conduct of the elections. It is also possible that if these parties are formed on ethnic and sectional lines they will operate in such a manner as to jeopardize national interest.

Multi party system may also make the formation of a new government very difficult. This is because a coalition government that assumes office after a multi party electoral contest lacks a common policy or platform before coming into power. It therefore forces on those parties in a coalition arrangement a lot of unhealthy compromises, horse-trading, concessions during which vital principles are abandoned, and ideological positions discarded for the sake of political patronage in a situation where merits are sacrificed on the altar of partisan gains that the system suffers. It may encourage bribery and corruption within the legislative arm due to the number of members from different parties to be lobbied before government programs and important legislations are passed in the parliament. The net effect of the combinations of this is to lower the quality of public policies and standard of public life. Most coalition governments that normally arise from multi party systems are often weak and unstable.

3.3.4 Zero-Party option

In very rare occasions, there are talks about a Zero or non-party system. This is one of the options that Gen. Muritala Muhammed (1939-1976), gave to the Constitution Drafting Committee (CDC) in Nigeria in 1975 when he charged the 50 'wise men' not to hesitate, during the course of their deliberation they found the means by which government can be formed without political parties, to recommend that alternative. The CDC members, however, did not found the Zero party option attractive as it dismissed it, in the following words, among others: "To accept a no-party system and yet accept some form of representative government would amount to accepting a *syndicalist* or *corporativist* political system. Were this even practicable, under modern conditions, it would not unlikely lead ultimately to a fascist system of government" (Graf, 1979:52).

Notwithstanding, in 1987, former President Babangida found it expedient to adopt the novel idea in the elections to the local government held during the year. However, it was not long before he discarded the idea and embraced that of party politics, in spite of its imperfections. One need to point out that it due to the problems associated with party politics that have made political leaders and politicians to, at one time or the other toy with novel idea of Zero party. Beyond this, we do not consider a Zero party system a conventional model in an ideal democratic system. What is acceptable in some matured democracies like the United States is idea of independent candidates. This idea also found favor with the Muhammed Uwais panel on electoral reforms in Nigeria. One may also add that the difference between the Zero party option and Independent candidacy is more of semantics than of substance.

Discuss which of the party system you think is the most suitable for the sustenance of democracy.

3.4   Functions of Political Parties

Worldwide political parties have been accepted as indispensable in a democratic political system. It is therefore important that we discuss their functions:

3.4.1 Popular Participation

Political parties promote popular political participation, make effective political choices in elections possible and facilitate the flow of public business in the legislature. Parties always state their positions on issues thereby arousing public sentiments and involvements. They also make candidates standing for elections on their tickets to identify with their platforms, and as result holding them accountable for their actions and inactions in government.

3.4.2 Representation

Political parties provide opportunities for representation. This refers to the capacity of parties to respond to and articulate the view of both members and the voters. In the language of system theory, political parties are major "inputting" devices that ensure that policies pursued by the government reflect the wishes of larger society. Since every society is composed of individuals and groups, not all of whom can participate directly in politics, political parties therefore provide these people, in varying combinations, avenue to participate indirectly in government. As the Italian Political Scientist, Giovanni Sartori has stated; parties are the central intermediate and intermediary structures between society and government"

3.4.3 Elite Formation and Leadership Recruitment

Parties of all kinds are responsible for providing democratic states with their political leaders. In most cases, parties provides a training ground for politicians, 159 equipping them with skills, knowledge and experience, which may be found useful in governance and goal formulation. Parties have traditionally been one of the means through which societies set collective goals. They play this role, because, in the process of seeking power, they help in formulating government policies and programs through their election manifestoes, campaigns, public debates, conferences, conventions, with a view to attracting popular support. The goal of a political party is to gain control of the government to enable it implement its electoral promises.

In a democracy political parties desire to gain and keep control of the government through the electoral process. It is therefore a misuse of the term to say political parties seek to capture power. That terminology crept into the Nigerian political lexicon due to the many years of military rule that has foisted a siege mentality on the psyche of Nigerian citizens.

3.4.4 Interest Articulation and Aggregation

In the process of developing collective goals, parties also help to articulate (express) and aggregate (combine) the various interests found in society. Parties, indeed, often develop as vehicle through which business; labor, religious, ethnic or other groups advance or defend their various interests. The fact that national parties invariably articulate the demands of a multitude of group forces them to aggregate these interests by drawing them together into a coherent whole, thereby balancing competing interests against each other.

3.4.5 Socialization and Mobilization

Through internal debates and discussions, as well as electoral campaigns and competitions, parties engage in political education and socialization. The issues they raise and articulate as well as the attitudes that are generated around them become part of the larger political culture of a country.

3.4.6 Organization of Government

It is often argued that complex modern societies would be ungovernable without political parties. Parties help in the formation of government. This is why we refer to the parliamentary system in Britain as party government because the policies and programs of the British government at any point in time are wholly based on the manifesto of the party that is power in the country. Parties give government a degree of stability and coherence especially if the members of the government are drawn from a single party. Parties also facilitate cooperation between the two major branches of government, the legislature and executive.

3.4.7 Avenue for Criticisms of Government policies

In the competitive environment of politics, political parties also serve as vital sources of opposition and criticisms, both inside and outside government. By broadening the space for political debates, they help in educating the electorates and ensure that government policies are more thoroughly scrutinized.

SELF-ASSESSMENT EXERCISE

Explain the roles of political parties in a democracy.

4.0   SUMMARY

In this unit, we have defined political parties, its structure and organization, its classification or types as well as the functions they perform. We also noted that political parties are indispensable in a democracy, because without it meaningful representation is not possible. We also observed that due to over two centuries of un- interrupted democratic order in developed countries such as Britain and the United States, party systems and politics have become institutionalized there compared to Third World countries like Nigeria and Egypt where party system are personalized, inchoate and largely reflect the primordial cleavages in these societies.

5.0   CONCLUSION

Political parties remain the only agency for obtaining and maintaining political power. As such, they must gain popular support, provide political leadership and respond to society's interests. Parties organize (or aggregate and articulate) public opinions and popular demand and communicate these to the decision making centers of government. Parties are therefore indispensable in a democratic political system. But the effectiveness of the party system will depend on the level of political culture in a country. In the advanced countries of the world such as the United States and Britain, the peoples have made a success of party systems. But in the developing climes such as Nigeria, party politics seem to have been fostering the cleavages and divisions within the society; hence the clamor by the citizens out of exasperation, especially in trouble periods, for the no party option, or even the extreme option of military intervention.

6.0   TUTOR-Marked ASSIGNMENTS

1.   Discuss the vital functions political parties perform in a political system
2.   Evaluate the role of two party systems to the success of the British parliamentary and the American presidential systems
3.   Explain the conditions that can make a country adopt a zero-party option.

UNIT 3   PRESSURE AND INTEREST GROUPS

1.0   Introduction
2.0   Objectives
3.0   Main Contents
    3.1   Definition and Functions of Pressure Groups
    3.2   Classification and Types of Pressure Groups
    3.3   Techniques employed by Pressure Groups to Influence Government
    3.4   Pressure Groups and Public Policy
    3.5   Differences between Pressure Groups and Political Parties
4.0   Summary
5.0   Conclusion
6.0   Tutor Marked Assignments

1.0   INTRODUCTION

This unit examines the role of pressure groups and other non-governmental, nonpartisan organizations in the political process. It also defines and classifies pressure groups into different categories based on the various functions they perform, as well as their permanent or ad-hoc mode of existence. The unit further discusses the role of pressure groups in engaging the government in policy formulation, or reevaluation, including the techniques that are at their disposal to influence government positively towards their interests or objectives. The unit finally made the basic distinction between pressure groups and political parties.

2.0   OBJECTIVES

At the end of this unit, you should be able to:

- define pressure groups in a manner that your definition(s) will bring out their importance as well as the role they play in the political process
- discuss how pressure groups can become an effective linkage mechanism with the government through a mixed and balanced use of the techniques that are available to them
- distinguish between political parties and pressure groups, without losing the advantage of how the two can collaborate to achieve the goals of a political system.

3.0   MAIN CONTENT

3.1   Pressure Groups

3.1.1 Definitions and functions

3.1.1.2 Perspectives on Pressure Groups

Pressure Groups are organized bodies, which seek to influence the context of government decisions. As an interest group, they seek to prevent government from initiating policies and programs, which they may consider to be unfavorable to the well-being of their members; or to influence government to fashion its policies to the best interest of their members. It is within the context of this particularistic approach to interest articulation, that some scholars have perceived pressure groups as "narrowly self-interested, out for themselves, (groups) without regard for the public good. James Madison in the *FEDERALIST* likened pressure or interest groups to factions "who are united and actuated by common impulse or passion, adverse to the rights of other citizens." In one breath, Madison suggested they should be outlawed, but in other breath, he conceded that "pressure groups are inevitable in a free society"; to try to eliminate them would require tyranny, a remedy worse than the disease".

We need to stress that interest groups and pressure groups are often used interchangeably; but they virtually convey the same meaning. While the emphasis in the former is on why a set of individuals aggregate in pursuit of a common goal in the latter, what is salient is the method they employ in pursuit their interest, which is usually by exerting pressure on agencies of government. The semantic similarities between pressure groups and interest groups was also affirmed by (Greenberg, 1993:215)" because efforts by the interest groups are often perceived by decisions makers as constituting pressures on them, so interest groups are often called pressure groups".

A pressure group in a democracy is any group of persons, which tries to get the government or other bodies to take notice of certain things or do something by bringing pressure to bear on such government or body. Thus, any organized group in a democratic system that tries to exert influence or lobbies for the benefit of its members is a pressure group. Here, the group is not presenting itself as a potential replacement for the existing government. Rather, it usually only seeks to pressurize government into taking a desired line of action. It is possible in certain cases, however, for a frustrated but powerful pressure group to openly support an opposition, in a desire to replace a party in power with the one more sympathetic to its cause.

A related concept is the concept of interest group organized around a particular interest for influencing public policy in regard of their interest. When local cement manufacturers in Nigeria once came together to seek to convince government to ban the importation of cement into the country, they become an interest group seeking to influence the public policy in the area of international trade. The difference between pressure group and interest group could be little more than a semantic one, since pressure group do form around one interest or the other while interest groups often need to exert pressure in order to influence government's policies in the direction they desired.

We can identify four factors that can help to explain the vibrancy or otherwise of pressure groups in a democracy. These include change in a nation's socio-economic and political structure and also in the international environment, which can create new interests, redefine or strengthen the old government policy itself. The presence of the required leadership outside government who are willing and able to use democratic means to organize a group for influencing government decisions and the policy directions of government. In this wise, that the more active a government is, the greater is the probability that more pressure groups will be formed around such activities.

3.3.3.3 Functions of Pressure Groups

Pressure groups are a vital part of a healthy democracy. Indeed the sustained and rapid expansion of pressure group activity and involvement in the political process is often seen as a sign of growing political involvement among the populace. Pressure groups perform the following functions:

(a)   Pressure groups promote discussion and debate, and mobilize public opinion on key issues. They also educate the public on specific issues. The Nigeria Labor Congress (NLC), Nigerian Bar Association (NBA) and the Nigerian Medical Association (NMA) have played prominent roles in this respect.

(b)   Pressure groups can also enhance democratic participation. They do this by articulating issues that political parties may not want to touch or dabble into.

They also provide an important access point for those who may want redress of their grievances. This may include providing a platform for the minorities who are marginalized from the mainstream of national politics, thereby lacking the means of directly representing themselves.

The Movement for the Survival of Ogoni People (MOSOP) has done this severally in   the long agitations by the minorities in Niger Delta in Nigeria for compensations on account of   environmental pollution, and for fiscal federalism Pressure groups can also   serve   as an important and valuable source of specialized information/expertise for the legislature and bureaucracy, who may have been overburdened by routine   activities and may not have the time' or even the expertise to handle certain issues. For example the Chambers of Commerce can make valuable inputs to the executive during budget preparations, and assist the legislators during public hearings and both arms in carrying out policy enrichments, in their several post- budget analyses.

(e) Pressure groups also play important role in pushing for policy changes or reversals, as well as forcing government's hands in making changes in implementation of public policies.

SELF-ASSESSMENT EXERCISE 1

Explain the roles of pressure groups in a political system.

3.2   Pressure Groups by classification and types

Pressure groups can be classified in two broad ways: either through the professions or careers of the members or the type of activities they engage in; or by their nature, character or life span. Depending on the objectives they seek to pursue, protect, promote or advance, pressure groups can be broadly categorized into three :- (a) Economic and Business pressure groups, such as the Nigerian Chamber of Commerce, Nigerian Employers Consultative Association (NECA), and Nigerian Association of Chamber of Commerce, Industries, Mines and Agriculture, (NACCIMA). The Nigerian Labor Congress (NLC) can conveniently be grouped under this category because, as a trade union as it is concerned with economic or labor related matters of wages, working conditions of workers and industrial disputes. These groups apply pressures on government to adopt favorable policies on taxation, tariff structure, interest rate and expatriate quotas.

The second category is composed of various professional groups such as the Nigerian Medical Association (NMA), The Nigerian Bar Association (NBA), and the Nigerian Union of Teachers (NUT). The third category is the religious pressure groups like the Supreme Council of Islamic Affairs (SCIA), Christian Association of Nigeria (CAN) etc. The second mode of broad classification can be of four different types: they include communal groups, institutional groups, associational groups and Anomic groups.

(a)   **Communal groups:** These are socio-cultural association whose membership are based on birth, rather than recruitment. They are part of the social institutions in a community, castes and ethnic groups such as the Arewa People's Congress (APC); the Odua People's Congress and the Ohaneze Indigbo all fall under this category.

(b)   **Institutional groups:** These are part of the machinery of government and they attempt to exert influence from within their organizations, using the government machinery. They are different from interest groups in that they enjoy no measure of autonomy or independence. Examples are civil servants, military officers and association of local government workers.

(c)   **Associational groups:** This group are formed by people who which to pursue shared, but limited goals. Groups as associations are characterized by voluntary action and the existence of common interests, aspirations or attitudes. The most obvious examples of associational groups are what are commonly called interest groups.

(d)   **Anomic groups:** These are groups that often emerge spontaneously in response to an issue and usually disperse after the objective has been achieved or when the contentious issues have been resolved. Examples of this type of groups include the Campaign for Democracy and the National Democratic Coalition that stood against the annulment of June 12, 1993 election under the Babangida and Abacha military regimes in Nigeria.

SELF-ASSESSMENT EXERCISE 2

State the major categories of Pressure groups that operate in your country.

3.3   Techniques and approaches by Pressure Groups

Several techniques are open to pressure groups to influence public policy making process. Lobbying of policy makers is the most popular or effective of these methods. This can be done in many ways. For instance, when a bill that is relevant to a pressure group comes before the legislature, the leadership of a pressure group may go directly to the lawmakers to solicit their support for, or against a bill before it becomes a law. The Nigerian Labor Congress in several instances has adopted this method. In advanced countries, pressure groups may employ the services of professional lobbyists in order to fully optimize the potential benefit of this method. Mobilization of members to either support or reject a particular government's policy is another method available to pressure groups. This is usually achieved through education of members on their policy preferences, or through publicity and propaganda in the mass media. By so doing, they would have succeeded in shaping a public opinion that would be favorable to their interests, and this will also influence policy makers in taking decisions. Pressure groups may also attempt to influence elections by appearing before party committees at party conventions, by making monetary contributions to candidates, or by offering propaganda services to candidates on the ticket of a party sympathetic to its interests. The idea behind this is that if such a party should come into power, it would adopt such policies that will be favorable to the pressure or interest group.

To be effective in influencing government policy, a pressure group may adopt any of these methods or a combination of them. However, pressure groups are conscious of the time to apply any of these methods in order to optimally achieve the desired effect. But the effectiveness of any of these methods will depend on the type of issues involved, the organizational strength or otherwise of the groups involved, the resources-human and material- at their disposal and their positions within the political, socio-economic structure of the country (Ajibola, 1978:133)

SELF-ASSESSMENT EXERCISE 3

Explain the most effective technique(s) available to Pressure groups to influence government's policies.

3.4   Pressure Groups and Policy Making Process

Public policy making is central to the activity of any government; especially a democratic government that is always conscious of justifying the mandate reposed in it by the electorates. If public policy is premised on goal attainment, or as Chandler and Plane defines it, "the strategic use of resources to alleviate national problems," then the process of making such policies is critical to the success or the failure of any government. But it is a fact that resources at the disposal of government in relation to the multiple, and often conflicting ends, or interests to be satisfied are limited. Based on Harold Lasswell's (1936) conception of politics as "who gets what, when and how and given the inadequacy of resources, government is thereby constrained to rank or prioritize these interests, in order to determine which one to address first. Therefore, a policy decision to solve an environmental, or political problem, may be at the expense of an economic or educational policy option.

Under this circumstance, pressure groups set in their own perception of socioeconomic problems and attempt to influence government about their own ideas of what constitute rational solutions, or options in the context of a rational decision-making. Adebayo (1982:89-90), identifies the following stages in decision making during which pressure groups can engage the government: when a given problem or demand is identified; when the nature of problem is determined by clarifying goals, value and objectives; the point at which the available possible choices of action are outlined; that stage when the probable cost and benefits of the alternatives course of actions are examined and considered; and the final point when policy makers select the option, which in their opinion, is most appropriate to maximize set goals. A proactive pressure group strategically positions itself and knows when and how best to influence policy making at any, or all of these stages.

The environments in which policy makers operate also have implications for the type of influence, which pressure groups can exert on policy-making. In a military setting where personal freedoms and liberty are curtailed, it may be difficult for pressure groups and other civil society organizations to enjoy smooth operation. Similarly, in advanced societies, where political campaigns are issue-oriented, policy makers are often favorably disposed to taking into account the competing views canvasses by interest groups. This is in contrast with developing societies like in Nigeria, where primordial factors, such as ethnicity and religion, or partisan considerations, are salient. Also, because pressure groups are usually urban-based, and given the nature of policy issues that are of interest to them, they are more likely to be concerned with issues of "first-order magnitude" that are either federal or state in nature, rather than local, or residual.

In most developing countries like Nigeria, the pre-occupation of policy makers has been with issues of economic development, political stability and social cohesion. Using Nigeria as a case study since the attainment of independence in 1960, we can identify key areas of public policy making in which different pressure groups have engaged the Federal Government.

3.4.1 The Anglo-Nigerian Defence Pact

The decision by the Balewa's government in 1962 to abrogate the Anglo-Nigerian Defence Pact, following demonstrations spearheaded by the students of University of Ibadan was a response by the government to a pressure group demand. Many Nigerian's felt the pact was an affront on Nigerian sovereignty. On the other hand, the insistence by the same government to go ahead with the Commonwealth Heads of State Conference in Nigerian in spite of the political disorder in the Western Region in January 1996 represents another extreme of the government's indifference or insensitivity to pressures from articulate and organized groups.

3.4.2 The Deregulation Policy of the Down Stream Sector

During his first term in office the Obasanjo's government decided to introduce what it called "appropriate pricing" for petroleum products in order to curb the smuggling of the products to neighboring countries and thus, maintaining price stability. The decision saw the price of petrol (PMS) jumping from N18:00 (the price the Obasanjo's administration inherited from its predecessor) to N70:00 within eight years, before President Yar'Adua reduced it to N 65:00. More than three times during President Obasanjo's administration, the Nigerian Labor Congress (NLC) went on strikes because it was not convinced about the government's stated rationale for the repeated increases. The Yar'Adua's administration also engaged the organized labor for dialogue aimed at convincing the body on its intention to completely remove the subsidies on petroleum products, in the name of total de-regulation of the down-stream sector.

3.4.3 ASUU and the case of 'Unilorin 34'

Since it entered into an agreement with the federal government in June 2001, the Academic Staff Union of Universities (ASUU) has been repeatedly calling on its members out on strikes to force the hands of the government to implement the terms of the pact. The agreement borders on issues of funding of universities, unpaid salaries and dismissal of 34 lecturers from the University of Ilorin. For about five months, almost all public universities in the countries were shut down in 2009, which completely disrupted the 2008/2009 academic session. The universities were only re-opened after the government agreed to substantially implement its agreement with ASUU. The Supreme Court in a landmark judgment in December 2009 also reinstated the sacked Unilorin lecturers.

3.4.4 The Derivation Policy

The age-long agitations by the oil producing states paid off when the Obasanjo's administration decided to set aside 13 percent to compensate the states for the ecological degradation and oil spillage arising from the exploratory activities of the oil companies. But this policy, in turn, created another problem of how to share the revenue among the littoral states which degenerate to a dilemma popularly known as on-shore, off-shore dichotomy. The search for a solution to this problem saw the oil bearing states converting to pressure groups, and finally instituted a legal suit for a judicial interpretation of the contentious law. The dispute was not resolved until the Supreme Court in its interpretation of the seaward boundaries of a littoral state abolished the so called on-shore, off-shore dichotomy. This forced the hands of the federal government to find a political solution to resolve the impasse.

SELF-ASSESSMENT EXERCISE 3

Mention some significant contributions of Pressure groups to public policy inputs in your country.

3.5   Pressure Groups vs. Political Parties

Although, pressure groups have much in common with political parties, the major difference is that pressures groups are not in contest for political power like the political parties. But because they fall within the general context of David Trumans's definition of "political interest groups", in pursuing their objectives, pressure groups may be involved in electoral process by endorsing candidates or shaping party's platforms. They, however, do not exceed, according to Truman, making certain claims upon other groups in the societies, by acting through or upon any of the institutions of governments" cited in (Ojo 1973:52).

We can summarize the differences between pressure groups and political parties as follows: While political parties seek to create change by being elected to public offices pressure groups attempt to influence public policies, and it may be through political parties or other linkage devises to get across to the government. Pressure groups are better able to focus on specialized issues whereas political parties tend to address a wide range of issues.

SELF-ASSESSMENT EXERCISE 4

Analyze the major distinctions between pressure groups and political parties.

4.0   SUMMARY

In this unit, we have discussed pressure groups and the role they play in influencing government policies in the direction of policies that favor them. We also examined different categories of pressure groups and the techniques that are available to enable them play their interface and linkage role within a political system. Lastly, with relevant examples we analyzed how pressure groups in Nigeria have engaged past governments in the country.

5.0　CONCLUSION

Pressure groups play very important role in any political system, especially in the area of complementing the activities of political parties. Without directly being in government, pressure groups in some societies have played decisive role not only in the making or re-making of policies, but also in the making and un-making of government. In Nigeria for example, pressure groups like the Nigerian Medical Association (NMA) under the leadership of the late Beko Ransome Kuti, the Petroleum and Natural Gas Senior Staff Association of Nigeria (PENGASSAN), under Comrade Frank Kokori, and the umbrella workers' union, the Nigerian Labor Congress (NLC), first under Hassan Sumonu and later, Comrade Adams Oshimhole have played major roles in influencing government policies. They engaged Nigerian governments either civilian or military. No one will deny that Oshimhole's ascension to the governorship seat in Edo State is due to the radical image he carved for himself as a labor leader.

6.0　TUTOR-MARKED ASSIGNMENTS

1. Compare the effectiveness of pressure groups under a democratic   dispensation with that of a military regime.
2. Examine the notion that lobbying is prone to corruption and justify its use as a weapon to influence public policies.
3. Discuss whether the pressure groups and political parties are birds of a feather.

UNIT 4   THE BRITISH POLITICAL SYSTEM

1.0   Introduction
2.0   Objectives
3.0   Main Contents
    3.1   The British constitution
    3.2   Formation and Working of Government
        3.2.1   The Role of the Prime Minister
        3.2.2   Parliamentary supremacy
        3.2.3   The cabinet
        3.2.4   The party system
    3.3   The British Monarchy
4.0   Summary
5.0   Conclusion
6.0   Tutor-Marked Assignments

1.0   INTRODUCTION

Is one political system that has survived for over three centuries, with its major planks remaining intact. Its resilience and capacity for endurance is best demonstrated in the manner the system has managed the transition from absolute to constitutional monarchy, without disrupting the fabric of the political system. This unit deals with the British system of government and discusses how its uniquely and largely unwritten constitution has firmly held the country's political system together. It also examines the place of the ceremonial monarch operating alongside a supreme Parliament and a cabinet, where the Prime Minister sits as primus inter pares, all firmly guided by age-long conventions, in which there is high level of national consensus and abiding constitutionalism.

2.0   OBJECTIVES

At the end of this unit, you should be able to:

- describe the basic features of the British unwritten constitution
- analyse the workings and organization of the cabinet system as a committee of the Parliament
- differentiate between the operations of the British Parliamentary system and the American Presidential system.

3.0   MAIN CONTENT

3.1   The British Constitution

3.1.1 Unwritten and Flexible

The British constitution is often described as an unwritten constitution. This is not to suggest that no part of the constitution is written down. On the contrary, some aspects of the British constitution such as the Magna Carter of 1215, the Petition of Rights of 1628 and the Bill of Rights of 1911 and other such enactments are written down. The Bill of Rights limited the powers of the English Monarch. More significantly, the unwritten character of the British constitution implies that at no time in the history of the country did the English people like the Americans at Philadelphia assemble to draft a constitution for their country. In addition, it also implies that the British constitution is not codified, or can be found in a single document, since some aspects of it like the examples we gave above are written, while other aspects like established conventions cannot be found in any known document. Other sources of the British constitution include statutes, judicial decisions and usages.

The British constitution is also usually described as flexible due to the simple and non complicated process of changing or amending it. Unlike the American constitution that is rigid because of its stringent amendment procedure the process of amending a constitution in Britain is like the simple process of making or annulling an ordinary law or statute.

3.1.2 Constitutional Conventions

It is however important to make a distinction between laws and conventions. While laws, by their statutory nature are enforceable in courts of law, this is not the case with conventions. Yet, given the manner conventions have evolved in Britain and their historical role as stabilizing mechanism for the conservative British society, it is rarely in the character of the British to violate these conventions. Let us examine some of these well-known conventions in order to demonstrate their enduring utility to the notable success of the British system. They include the understanding that the first among equals in the cabinet is the Prime Minister who is the leader of the party having a majority in the House of Commons. Members of the cabinet are appointed and dismissed by the Parliament; Ministers with cabinet rank are selected from the majority party; policies pursued by the cabinet are consistent with the program of the party given the mandate by the electorate; and there must be support of the House of Commons for government policies including the norm that cabinet members must sit in either the House of Common or Lords.

Other conventions include the requirement that peerage may be created from outsiders to enable them participate in cabinet deliberations but such step can only be taken if the post does not excite controversy:

- A government defeated on a major issue must resign
- A government resigns if defeated at a general election
- Parliament stands dissolved on the request of the Primary Minister Should a government be defeated at the polls, the Prime Minister tenders his resignation on behalf of the government without meeting the new Parliament in which, lacking a majority, he would face an immediate defeat.
- The Prime Minister and his/her cabinet ministers should resign if a vote of no confidence is passed on the government.
- The principle of collective responsibility presumes that both the Prime Minister and his/her cabinet ministers are collectively responsible to the Parliament.

3.1.3   Unitary System of Government

Britain operates a unitary system of government. Under this arrangement, all governmental powers are concentrated at the central level. Any local level of government that exists are created and allocated powers by the central government. This is unlike the United States where the states as federating units derive their powers from the constituents, and are equal, exercising co-ordinate authority with the federal government in those powers allotted to them.

SELF-ASSESSMENT EXERCISE 1

Explain the importance of conventions to the enduring stability of the British government.

3.1.4   Formation and Workings of Government

3.2.5 The Role of the Prime Minister

The British Prime Minister is the head of government and the country's political leader. His functions can be seen from his role in the formation of the government, in giving direction to the cabinet, in sustaining majority in the parliament and as the Monarch's principal adviser. The Prime Minister is at the center of these bodies and personalities and he must work in cooperation with them to ensure the success of the state. It is important that you know his major functions which include the following:

3.2.2 Prime Minister and Power of appointments

The Prime Minister has wide powers of patronage including the appointment and dismissal of Ministers. For example in 1962 Harold Macmillan, conservative P. M. dismissed a third of his cabinet overnight. In this age when "professional" politicians predominate, the Prime Minister's ability to affect directly the careers of ambitious members of Parliament for good or bad is crucial. He appoints all Ministers, promotes, demotes or dismisses them. He also assigns portfolio or responsibilities to each of them; thereby deciding who does what in cabinet. The Prime Minister also appoints Chairmen of Cabinet committees, which have now become increasingly important in the operations of the British government

3.2.3 Prime Minister and Direction of the Cabinet

Chooses Cabinet and determines its size. He summons meetings, determines agenda, sums up the "mood" of meetings, approves minutes, and cabinet spoke man to the outside world

3.2.4 Prime Minister and Parliament

He is the leader of parliament since his party commands majority in the House of Commons and one of his functions is to constrain the activities of the opposition, co-ordinates parliamentary party caucuses to enable his party continue to retain majority and manages Question Time in such a way that the government is not embarrassed.

3.2.5 Prime Minister and Party

He is the leader of the party that forms the government; and exercises a major influence on government policies

3.2.6 The Prime Minister and the Monarch

He advises the sovereign on the appointment of important officials and on the granting of honors. The Prime Minister personally advises the monarch on the date of the dissolution of Parliament and this matter is not discussed in the Cabinet.

3.2.6.1 Parliamentary system of government/Parliamentary Supremacy

The Parliamentary system of government was first developed in Britain and the British government today still provides the best example of that form of administration. It is a system of dual executive in which there is a division between the head of state (the Monarch) and the head of government (the Prime Minister).The parliament is the supreme legislative body in Britain. This primacy of the parliament has even been expressed in seeming hyperbolic sense that it is so supreme that it can turn a man into a woman. But in a less epigrammatic sense this supremacy is true to the extent that no Act of Parliament in Britain can be declared unconstitutional; a situation that has made scholars to describe the Parliament in Britain as the country's constitution.

In Britain members of the executive and the smaller cabinet are selected from the parliament. In other words, membership of the parliament is a pre condition for an appointment into the cabinet, a practice that gives no room for separation of powers as it operates in the United States. Members of the parliament are partly elected (the Commons) and selected (the Lords). Also, elections into the Parliament are held every five years or earlier if the government is defeated on a major policy issue, a vote of no confidence is passed by the parliament on the executive, or if in the opinion of the monarch, the Prime Minister no longer have sufficient majority in the House of Commons to carry through government programs.

It is important that you know the major features of the British parliamentary system of government as we outline below:

- The British Parliamentary system of government comprises two chambers i.e. the House of Commons, the lower and the House of Lords, the upper chamber.

- The head of government, the Prime Minister is not popularly elected. The Prime Minister by convention is usually the leader of the party that controls the majority of seats in the parliament. Presently, Mr. Gordon Brown is the British Prime Minister, since his party, the Conservative has the majority in the House of Commons. He succeeded Mr. John Major of the same party.

- The head of government exercises the executive functions of government in Britain, and he chooses his ministers from his party men in the legislature.

- In Britain, the Prime Minster and his Ministers who are members of the executive are also part of the legislature. There is therefore fusion of powers between the executive and the legislative arms.

The principle of collective responsibility is also observed in Britain.

This implies that members of the executive are collectively responsible for any decision taken by them. The implication of this principle is that they all share the blame or glory for the failure or success of any decision taken by the government of the day.

- In the British government, there is also the existence of official and legally recognized opposition Party. The party that has the second highest vote in the parliament forms the shadow cabinet, whose responsibility is to offer better alternatives to the programs of the government of the day, as well as constructive criticisms to the opposition party.

- A vote of no confidence: The executive can be removed from office by the legislature if a vote of no confidence is passed against the executive.

Party discipline or obedience to the directives of the party is another feature of the British system. In other words, members of the ruling party are expected to obey party directives once they have been decided upon, since the success and failure of the government depend on the ability of members of the ruling party to stick together. This job is usually performed by the party whip who is to ensure that members do not stray from the official position of the party on major policy issues.

- All cabinet members are Ministers, but not all Ministers are cabinet members.

These characteristics and requirements, as well as their observance are important for the cabinet, being a committee of the parliament to maintain its integrity in order for the government to remain focused in the implementation of the party's platform, upon which it was voted into power by the electorates.

3.2.6.2 The Cabinet

Writing in 1867, Walter Bagehot, in *The English Constitution* declared that the two characteristic features of Cabinet Government in Britain were, firstly, that the cabinet is a collective executive body, and secondly, that it is drawn from Parliament and answerable to Parliament (rather than directly to the electorate) for its authority and very existence. This, argued Bagehot, is in direct contrast with Presidential system in the United States of America where the executive is the single figure of the President, who is elected directly by the people and thus not responsible to the legislature. The traditional description of the Prime Minister's role in the cabinet is that of *"primus inter pares,"* but it is widely claimed today that the power of the Prime Minister within the cabinet is so decisive and significant that he is more than 'first among equal'.

3.3   Functions

The role of cabinet is that of a central directing force within the machinery of government, making the important decision of policy, supervision the execution of that policy, in general and co-coordinating the work of the whole executive machine. We can summarize the functions of the cabinet as follows:

1.   It draws up policy, fills in the detail of policy,
2.   Takes decision when the various items shall be submitted to Parliament,
3.   Determines policies to be followed in response to the pulse of the nation or current challenges,
4.   Co-ordinates policies, supervises the work of the executive and draws up plans for the future.

3.4   Composition

In essence, the Cabinet has always been a collection of departmental heads. This has the advantage that members can bring administrative expertise to policy decisions. The two, it is argued, are inseparable. With this in mind, the Prime Minister has to consider and balance a number of factors when forming his Cabinet. If too many ministers are included in the cabinet it becomes an unwieldy body, and conflict with the general principle that the task of decision-making is most effectively performed by a small body. If too few ministers are included, it becomes difficult for the cabinet keep in touch with the other members of the government-back-benchers and the party outside Parliament.

Some departmental posts such as Foreign Secretary, Home Secretary, and Chancellor of the Exchequer would be included in any conventional Cabinet. Posts like Lord Privy Seal, Lord President of the Council, and Chancellor of the Duty of Lancaster can be included in the Cabinet in order that their holders may perform non-departmental functions and can therefore undertake the tasks of policy coordination, long-term planning, and general administrative functions. Personality factors inevitably play a vital part in cabinet making. The Prime Minister has to include among his ministers individuals of standing within the party, regardless of their potential ministerial ability. This is particularly important when it is considered that a number of diverse elements exist within the British parties.

The Prime Minister also has to decide whether a particular party extremist would be a biggest threat to party unity in or out of the Cabinet, in that sometimes possible to "buy" silence and conformity from a potential rebel by giving him the responsibility of ministerial office. This is what Clement Attlee did when he included Aneurin Bevan in his cabinet, and the inclusion of Cousin in Wilson's.

3.5   Party system in Britain

According to Maurice Duverger (1964), the party system is at the centre of the British parliamentary government: "The party holds in its own hands the essential prerogatives of the Legislature and the Executive. Government posts are in the hands of its leaders who apply its doctrine and its program as expressed in its electoral "platform..." In Britain, the Party with majority in the parliament wields considerable power; it is entitled to form a government while the other party forms the opposition government, or the shadow cabinet. The labor party under the leadership of Gordon Brown presently forms the government in Britain while the Conservatives are in opposition. These two parties have been alternating in government for close to a century, and have in between them produced world class Tory Prime Ministers such as Winston Churchill and Margret Thatcher, as well as Labor Premiers like, Harold Wilson and Tony Blair.

SELF-ASSESSMENT EXERCISE 2

Describe the role of the Prime Minister in both the cabinet and the parliament.

3.6   The British Monarchy

The monarchy in Britain is a hereditary institution which parliament regulates by the rules of succession. The Act of Settlement of 1701 and the Statute of Westminster of 1931 are major laws in Britain governing the appointments and powers of the King/Queen of England. The monarchy is the symbol of the continuity of the British government. It is an integral part of the Parliament, the sovereign that makes the monarch not answerable to any court in Britain and thereby not liable to arrest.

The powers of the monarch include giving assent to bills before they become laws and enforcement of national laws. The normal recital of Acts of Parliament: "Be it be enacted by the Queen's most Excellent Majesty, by and with the advise and consent of the Lords Spiritual and Temporal, and Commons..." confirms the powers of the monarch in every legislation in parliament. The monarch also appoints Prime Ministers, summons, prorogues or dissolves parliament, and reads the address from the throne at the opening of parliament. But in exercising these powers, the monarch by convention relies on the advice of the Parliament since the King or Queen cannot do, or be permitted to do any wrong ever. The monarch or the sovereign as Walter Bagehot puts it, has three rights-the right to be consulted, the right to encourage, the right to warn"; and he concluded: "A King of great sense and sagacity would want no others" With this type of arrangement, the sanctity of the monarchy is preserved by ensuring that for every act of the monarch there is someone responsible to the parliament. The monarchy is a highly respected institution in Britain, because it provides for the continuity of the British government. According to Peel, "a King after a reign of ten years ought to know much more of the machine of government than any other man in the country." In spite of the powers ascribed to the King in Britain, the tradition is that the king does not govern, but reign. For this reason, monarchy in Britain does not constitute an encumbrance to democracy or the popular will. The evolution of constitutional monarchy in Britain was meant to prevent the institution from obstructing the wheel of democracy.

SELF-ASSESSMENT EXERCISE 3

Explain the meaning of the phrase "The King reigns but does not rule"

4.0   SUMMARY

In this unit we discussed the British system of government, especially how it evolved from absolute and unlimited to a constitutional monarchy. We noted that Britain operates an unwritten, flexible and unitary constitutional structure. We also identified the cabinet as a committee of a supreme parliament, both headed by a Prime Minister who exercises real executive powers, alongside a titular monarch whose power is more symbolic and ceremonial, than substantive. Yet this delicate arrangement of grafting monarchy with democracy has endured for so long due to the unique British tradition of respect of age long conventions and almost infinite capacity for adaptation to modern changes.

5.0   CONCLUSION

The British Parliamentary system of government has advertised itself because of its several advantages. However, like every other human arrangement, it has thrown up its own weaknesses, yet its success story in Britain has encouraged other nations to look at the United Kingdom with envy, to the extent that some have copied the system while others are looking into the possibility of adopting some aspects of it. Unlike the American presidential system, the British political system has been reputed to be more sensitive to the opposition and public opinion and responsible to the electorate, offers prospects for more accountable government flexible enough to cope with changing mood of the nation, and above all less expensive to operate.

6.0   TUTOR-MARKED ASSIGNMENTS

1.   Identify the major reasons for the success of the British Parliamentary System of government
2.   Explain why the concept of parliamentary supremacy is at the heart of the British Government.
3.   Critically examine the role of the Prime Minister in Britain as *primus inter pares*, with that of a Supreme Parliament and a Sovereign Queen.

UNIT 5   AMERICAN POLITICAL SYSTEM

1.0   INTRODUCTION

The United States is variously and famously described as the "New World", "God's Own Country", The Promised Land" and a Melting Point, the latter, due to the remarkable success of its assimilation policy. This unit examines the American political system, which is based on a two party structure, an executive President who shares his powers with no individual, except the Congress, a body separately elected, and which under the doctrine of separation of powers, has specific, principally, legislative functions assigned to it by the constitution.

2.0   OBJECTIVES

At the end of this unit, you should be able to:

- examine the background to the United States present constitutional arrangement.
- explain the difference between the confederal arrangement in the USA before 1787 and the present federal structure in the country today.
- analyse how the doctrines of Separation of Powers and Checks and balances combine to prevent abuse of power and promote a responsive government in the country.

3.0   MAIN CONTENT

3.1   Historical background

The United States of America is a former colony of Great Britain. In 1776, Americans fought the war of liberation. A committee appointed by the Second Continental Congress headed by Thomas Jefferson drafted the American Declaration of Independence. The Declaration was an extra-ordinary document both in philosophical and political terms. Philosophically, it proclaimed all men were created equal and asserts that certain rights- including life, liberty and the pursuit of happiness are inalienable, and could not be abridged by government. At a time when most Kings in Europe were claiming divine right to rule, this was a remarkable statement. Politically, despite the differences that divided the Northern merchants and Southern planters, the declaration was able to focus on problems, grievances, aspirations and principles that seemed to unify them.

According to John Adams, who wrote of American Revolution: "The men who made it wanted not just independence, but a change that would transform their own societies, and set a new example for mankind. Though the United States faced the first challenge to her unity under President Abraham Lincoln, yet it was settled that the state would continue to play the central role in the American Revolution of ideas, and it would be within the state arena that the republican experiment would be conducted. In line with the inscription under the statue of liberty: "liberty lightening the World," Americans are said to prefer freedom to equality, and proudly refer to their country as the "Promised Land". The United States is a melting pot of several nationalities that migrated across the Atlantic due to, among other reasons, religious persecution.

In the early days of American nation, the country engaged in unbridled expansionism. From (1776 to 1976) for instance, the US expanded from an enclave of thirteen states on the Atlantic Seaboard to a continental power extending into the Pacific (King, 1977:154). In territory from 1776 to 1939 when World War II broke out, the area under US domination increased from 400,000 square miles to 3,738,393 square miles. In 77 years alone, (1776-1853) the US expanded across the continent with an area of 300 miles from East to West, and more than 1500 miles from North to South. This accretion in US territory from Louisiana, which increased American territory by about 50 percent, to Florida, which was ceded from Spain, in pursuit of President Andrew Jackson's doctrine of "manifest destiny," was achieved by a combination of military expedition, diplomatic maneuvers, and in some cases, outright purchase.

SELF-ASSESSMENT EXERCISE

Explain why the United States is described as a melting point.

3.2   American Confederal Constitutional Structure

The United States of America proclaimed itself an independent country in 1776 after a War of Independence led by George Washington who later became the first President of the country. The former thirteen colonies eventually became the pioneer confederal states that formed the United States of America. The Articles of Confederation and Perpetual Union was adopted in November 1777 and was operated until March 1789. As provided for under Article II "each state retains its sovereignty and independence, and every power, jurisdiction and right, which is not by this confederation expressly delegated to the United States, in Congress assembled." From this provision, it is obvious that the Articles of Confederation was concerned primarily with limiting the powers of the central government; and this it did in the following ways:

a.   The central government was based entirely on the Congress
b.   There was no Executive branch of government
c.   Execution of laws passed by the Congress was left to the discretion of individual states
d.   Members of the Congress were no more than delegates, or messengers from the states; and they could be recalled by the states at will
e.   Congress also lacked the powers to levy tax
f.   Although Congress had power to declare war, there was no central army; the central government could only rely on state militia.

Due to these limiting provisions, the confederal arrangement was unable to hold the nation together. As a voluntary compact of sovereign states in which the central government lacked legal authority to enforce compliance with the laws the arrangement was doomed to fail. Added to these constitutional inadequacies was the lack of trust among the states. The Annapolis Convention, which held because of an invitation from the Virginia legislature, was the first major attempt to revise the Articles of Confederation. But it was not very successful as only delegates from five states attended the convention. It took the bloody Shay's Rebellion for the Founding Fathers to commit themselves to a major review of the Articles of Confederation Americans

SELF-ASSESSMENT EXERCISE 2

Examine the factors that led to the collapse of confederation in the United States.

3.3 Adoption of a Federal Constitution by the US

In order to escape the strain under which the United States operated, the American founding fathers convened a Constitutional Convention at Philadelphia, which was attended by delegates from the states. The conference was dominated by a heated debate before it settled for a federal constitution as the most suitable for the country. The major debate centered on how to reconcile the divergent Virginia Plan and the New Jersey Plan. The Virginia Plan provided for a system of representation in the national legislature based on the population of each state or the proportion of each state's revenue contribution, or both. The New Jersey Plan, on the other hand, concentrated on specific weaknesses in the Articles of Confederation, in the spirit of revision, rather than a complete replacement of the document. In the end an agreement, popularly called the "Connecticut Compromise" was reached. In the Great Compromise the Constitutional Conference of 1787 gave each state an equal number of senators regardless of its population, but allocated representation in the lower house on the basis of population Apart from promoting unity in diversity, one of the reasons why the United States opted for a federal system is to strengthen the capacity of the nation to declare war and protect the states against foreign intrusion. From the federalist papers co-authored by Paul Hamilton, John Jay and James Madison, as well as the foundation laid by the Founding Fathers like George Washington and Thomas Jefferson, one is left in doubt as to the character of the American nation and the direction it would go. The American constitution is often seen as an inspired, if not divine work, expressing timeless principles of democratic government. The American system of government, which draws its strength from its federal constitutional arrangement, has been so successful that many countries in the world have either grafted portions of American system into their own political structures, or transplanted wholesale the US model, thereby conferring on it a constitutional orthodoxy. Countries such as Australia, Canada, Germany, Switzerland and Nigeria borrowed the major planks of their constitution from the American experience, a country widely recognized to have the patent or franchise for federalism.

Federalism was adopted in the United States as a step towards greater centralization of powers. The delegates agreed that they needed to place more powers at the national level without completely undermining the state governments. Thus, a system of dual sovereigns was devised- the state and the nation-with the hope that competition between the two would be an effective limitation on the power of both. The United States is also a federal republic, and according to James Madison, a republic refers to a government of elected representatives of the people, having no room for a king. Being slightly democratic but highly republican, US citizens do not have a great of formal control over their political system. In view of its diversity, pluralism rather than pure democracy is a more suitable term to describe the American system. Madison was of the view that a country as geographically large and as economically, socially, politically and culturally diverse as the United States cannot with ease attains a single majority on most issues. Because the American people have been called a nation of joiners, individuals must join with the other people to achieve his or her political goals.

The US federal constitution today remains arguably the most enduring political document in the world; it is often described as a masterpiece having been a product of an ingenious constitutional engineering. At the beginning, the constitution was concerned with structure and powers of government. The next stage was the passage of the Bill of Rights on the insistence of George Mason, Thomas Jefferson and Samuel Adams. Later franchise or voting right was extended to almost every adult male under Andrew Jackson. The Abraham Lincoln era liberated the slaves and promulgated Homestead Act, which made free land available to poor farmers. The progressive era amended the constitution to give women voting rights. The New Deal under Franklin Delano Roosevelt brought social security, collective bargaining and social welfare, while the era of the Great Society under John Kennedy and Lyndon Johnson launched a war on poverty and racism (Baradat, 2000).

Let us now take a closer look at the major features of the US's constitution.

3.4   Major features of U.S. Constitution

3.4.1 A strong Executive President

The United States' constitution under Article II provided for the establishment of the office of a strong president. As pointed out by Alexander Hamilton, a popular delegate to the 1787 Constitutional Convention, Article II was aimed towards "energy in the Executive." It did so in an effort to overcome the natural stalemate that was built into the bicameral legislature as well as into the separation of powers among the three organs of government. The President of the United States exercises Executive powers as the Head of State; Head of government and Commander-in-Chief of the Armed forces. As Sir, Henry Maine aptly puts it: "The King of England reigns but does not govern; the French President neither reigns nor governs; the American President governs, though (not being a king) he does not govern" (Appadorai, 2004).

The powers and authority of an American president remains single and undivided. Stephen Skowronek (2002: xiv) wrote of the oval office in America thus: "The Presidency has been a singularly persistent source of change, a transformative element engrained in the constitution itself. In the presidency change is generated by incumbents trying to legitimate themselves." His ministers (known as secretaries), who are largely chosen by him are therefore not his colleagues but mere advisers, and he is not bound by their advice. Unlike in Britain, the concept of collective responsibility does not apply to the American system. What keeps the system going is the combined application of the principle of separation of powers and the doctrine of checks and balances.

3.4.2 Division of Powers

Cooperative and political inter-dependence among states in US prohibits the centre from certain things e.g. prohibit states religion, cannot suspend right of habeas corpus. The constitution prohibits the state from entering into a treaty or confederation or community. Residual powers – powers not delegated to the federal government nor prohibited to the states are reserved to the states respectively or to the people. The constitution recognizes a second tier system of fifty state governments, with a strong constitutional base and significant formal power in revenue and taxation, inter-state commerce, health, education, etc, but with a history of uneven utilization of these powers. All this are made to work by an American citizenry- richly diverse in ethnic, racial, class and regional terms that historically have distrusted government, but show patriotism to their country.

3.4.3 Separation of Powers:

The United States' constitution also incorporates the principle of separation of powers and checks and balances among the three organs of government. In a brilliant formulation, Richard Neustadt (1960:13) described separation of Powers as a system not of separated powers but of "separated institutions sharing power." S .E Finer (1949) also stated that the American constitution was consciously and elaborately made an essay in the separation of powers and is today "the most important polity in the world which operates upon the principle. By dividing the Congress into two bodies, the Senate elected for six years term with partial renewal after two years, and the House biennially, and by vesting legislative, executive and judicial functions in separate organs, the American constitution aimed at diminishing the chance that power will be misused.

3.4. 4 Checks and Balances

This is a mechanism through which each branch of government in USA is able to participate in and influence the activities of the other branches. Its major examples include the power of the President to veto Congressional legislations, the Senate's power to confirm presidential appointments and the power of the Judiciary to review laws enacted by the Congress. According to Ray (2006: 145) the primary objective of the Federalist Papers for instituting the doctrine of checks and balances was "to provide for an equilibrated system of interaction among the three principal institutions of the executive, the legislature and the judiciary". Indeed, the doctrine of checks and balances is recognition of the reality in the process of government: To run a government, powers must not only coordinate, they must also overlap.

3.4.5 Bicameral National Legislature

The Senate has 100 members elected based on equality of states while 436 members of the House of Representatives are elected based on population, in which a single member constituency of about 30,000 voters sends a representative to the lower chamber. The two independent national legislative chambers have different constituencies and frequently bi-partisan, reflecting divergent views on federal state-local relations. The equal representation in the Senate seeks to balance bigness and smallness, majority rule and majority rules, centralizing and decentralizing tendencies.

3.4.6 Judicial Review

This is the Power of the court to render legislative and executive acts null and void if they violate the constitution. The Supremacy Clause covers the judicial role in resolving inter-governmental disputes that may arise as a result of inconsistent state legislations. Where such arise, the Supreme Court has the power to declare a state's legislation that is inconsistent with federal laws null and void, while that of the federal government remains valid.

3.4.7 Two- Party System

The government of the United States operates on two-party system: the two political parties are Democratic and Republican Parties. This does not suggest that there are only two political parties in the country. Rather only two parties are strong enough to alternate in government. It is believed that party competition contribute to the health of the American democratic process, especially the bi- partisan consensus that often shape the country's electoral process. Thus, it is not unusual for one party to control the Presidency, while the other party dominates the Congress, or an arm of it. In the early years of the Republic, the idea of party competition was not that warmly accepted. In 1798, the Federalist Party, which controlled the national government, sought to outlaw the Democratic-Republican opponents through the Alien and Sedition Acts. But the attempts failed. Also, in the 19th Century, American politics was dominated by powerful party machines. However, this has given way in modern times to candidate-centered electoral politics in which individual candidates have taken over campaign organization and voters mobilization.

3.5 Amendment Procedure

The American constitution is often described as a rigid constitution to indicate the difficult and cumbersome procedure that the process entails. In defense of this, James Madison argued that the method was to guard "equally against the extreme facility which would render the constitution too mutable and that extreme difficulty which might perpetuate discovered faults". In spite of this complicated procedure, in over two hundred years of its operations the U.S.'s constitution has been amended for about twenty five times. The first amendment legally secure freedom of speech and of peaceful assembly; the fourth amendment forbids a search without a warrant, the fifth amendment replaced the word right to pursuit happiness with right to property; the eight amendment legally secures the citizen against excessive bail, while the fourteenth amendment prohibits discrimination against any citizen of the United States on the basis of color (Laski 19 103).

SELF-ASSESSMENT EXERCISE 3

Explain why a federal constitution is most suitable for the Federal Republic of Nigeria.

3.6   Presidential System of Government

Though a former colony of Britain, U.S.A. turned her back on the monarchical system for which Britain is renowned and embraced a republican presidential democracy. For over two hundred years now, the United States has made a success of her presidential system of government, anchored on a two party, and strengthened by a bi-partisan consensus, an arrangement that has not only promoted political stability in the country, but has also assured for the Americans unprecedented level of economic prosperity. Under the Presidential system of government, the President who has the whole country as his constituency is elected separately for a fixed term of four years, and separately from the Congress. The President is the head of state, head of government and commander-in-chief of the armed forces. But in some respects despite having the whole country has his constituency, the President in exercising his major functions of legislations, appointments; treaty making and declaration of war shares his power with the Congress. This is why Baradat (2000) described the US's government as "a Presidential-Congressional system", which he labeled "a divided government". The import of the so-called "divided government" came into light when in 1919 the President and the Senate disagreed and went separate ways over the Versailles Peace Treaty, a row that prevented the United States from joining the League of Nation

SELF-ASSESSMENT EXERCISE

Explain the major features of the presidential system of government.

4.0   SUMMARY

In this unit, we have discussed the origins of the American presidential System of government. We outlined the reasons that led to the failure of the confederal constitution after it was operated for about a decade and two years. We also stated the reasons why the Founding Fathers opted for a federal constitution in 1787. The Unit also discussed the positive contributions of the two party systems to the success of the American political model, as well as the combined roles of the principles of Separation of Powers and Checks and balances in curbing executive lawlessness and ensuring good governance, under a presidential system of government.

5.0   CONCLUSION

In over two hundred years the American political system has been tested by several challenges, but it has endured and remained resilient. In the early years of the republic, the political system was able to withstand the trauma and strain of a civil war. In the first half of the 20th century, it also withstood the challenges posed by two World Wars, in addition to those of the Great Depression. The Supreme Court, by exercising its power of judicial review or invoking the supremacy clause has also amicably resolved the irregular electoral disputes, and has maintained the delicate balance between the federal government and the fifty federating units (states). Despite the divisive impact of the civil rights movements, the American political system has now matured that the civil rights challenges were eventually resolved that today an African American, Barrack Obama is now the occupant of the White House in Washington.

6.0   TUTOR-MARKED ASSIGNMENTS

1.   Compare and contrast the American presidential and the British parliamentary systems of government
2.   Evaluate the roles of the   twin concepts of Separation of Powers and Checks and   Balances to the success   of the Nigerian democracy.
3.   Assess the major achievements of the federal system of government in over two centuries of its adoption in the United States.

UNIT 6   ELECTORAL SYSTEM AND PROCESS

1.0   INTRODUCTION

The electoral system is the heart of any democratic system. For this reason most democratic states are conscious of the imperative to put in place a good electoral system that will ensure free and fair elections. This unit begins with what is meant by an electoral system as well as the different types of electoral systems. It also discusses the conditions that are to be met to achieve free and fair elections and an overview of the electoral process in Nigeria, from the colonial period till date.

2.0   OBJECTIVES

At the end of this unit, you should be able to:

- explain the meaning and types of electoral system.
- analyse the conditions that are necessary to achieve free and fair elections.
- discuss the history of the electoral systems/administration in Nigeria.

3.0   MAIN CONTENT

3.1   Definition and types of an electoral system

All modern democratic nations in the world have evolved a system by which their citizens participate in the process of electing their leaders. It is through elections that people express their views on issues and accord legitimacy to, or withdraws it from, political leadership. J. J. Rousseau, who popularized the doctrine of the "general will" preferred direct democracy to representative government, since according to him, "individuals will could not be transferred because it is inalienable, and that no one can adequately represent another individual (Baradat, 2000:82). But today direct democracy is no longer realistic because the world has advanced beyond the Greek city states. Therefore, what is now popularly referred to as liberal democracy rest on the pillars of representative government, universal suffrage and unrestricted franchise or voters' eligibility.

The electoral system is a process or the machinery through which citizens in any given democratic state elect their representatives in competitive elections that are held at periodic intervals. While the casting of vote is the highest point of an electoral process, other activities are involved before the process can said to be complete. An essential task of an electoral system is to provide opportunity for a broad spectrum of the citizens to participate in the political process. This is very significant in any type of government, unitary or federal, but more so, in the latter, because a good electoral system help to foster national integration. Broadly, an electoral system may either be based on the majority rule or Proportional Representation system.

3.1.1 Majority rule system

In a majority rule system that is practiced in Nigeria at present, the party or candidate with the majority of votes cast in an election is declared the winner. But a major disadvantage of majority rule system is that a party may win a minority of votes, and nevertheless command majority of seats in parliaments, and thus form a government. Another party may win less than half of the seats, but with disproportionately high margin of votes. This oddity of the majority-rule variant of an electoral system may be tolerated where it occurs occasionally, but where it occurs more frequently, it certainly poses grave danger to the polity. Also in a majority rule system, the minority parties that are constantly defeated at elections may either lose interest in politics, or develop radical or subversive ideas. It may also encourage the fragmentation of Political parties along regional or ethnic lines. This scenario is true of Nigerian politics in the defunct first republic (Sklar; 1963). In a single member constituency as long as there are more than one candidate for a single seat in an election, the seats will always be distributed among political parties disproportionately to the votes cast. Two illustrative cases are relevant here. In the 1992 general election in Britain, the Conservative Party led by John Major secured a majority of seats in the parliament, but the party failed to win a majority of popular votes (Baradat, 2000:132). Also, if we use a simulative scenario of an election involving three parties, and in which the distribution of votes is as follows: Party A, 41%; Party B, 39% and Party C, 29%, it is obvious that Party A, with 41 percent has won. Yet majority of voters (59 percent) voted against party A, and therefore that huge percentage of voters are unrepresented. In quantitative terms, 41 percent of the voters won 100 percent of representation. The implication therefore is that all those who voted for party B or C might as well have stayed away from the election since their votes do not count. This is why the majority rule system, is generally criticized for promoting the winner takes all, or zero-sum syndrome.

3.1.2 Proportional Representation

Under the system of proportional representation, however elections are not decided at constituency level. The country as a whole is considered as one single consistency and the various parties present candidates to the entire electorate on lists, and voters are expected to choose from those lists. A party will therefore be allotted in parliament as many seats as correspond to the percentage of votes scored in the entire country. The parliament is, therefore, a reflection of the strength of each party based on the number of votes. Under this variant, government is usually, if not always, by a coalition of several parties. Its major advantage is that it is evidently more just than majority system, because it provides room for more parties to participate in government, and thus prelude the possibility of instability arising from the injustice because of consistent exclusion of minority parties from government. Its major defect is that it encourages the proliferation of small parties that may eventually win not so significant number of seats in parliament, and may make the process of forming a stable government difficult.

A case in point is the German (1919) constitution where not less than forty-two parties contested for elections and in the election not more than fourteen of those parties, managed to win seats in parliament (Kriele 1979:357). Also, the Salvador Allende government of 1970 was a coalition of the major political parties in Chile. But when the controversies over redistribution of farmlands and their nationalization assumed irreconcilable level among the coalition partners, the various parties withdrew their support. To avert a deadlock, Allende abandoned all democratic pretences and became dictatorial; the army intervened, and he was subsequently murdered in 1973 (Baradat2000:135). It is the realization that none of these two variants is perfect that led some scholars to suggest a modification of the two, to achieve what has been called a "mixed-system," such as the tripe mandate system or the minority-quorum system (Kriele, 1979:359).

Whether in a majority rule or proportional system, representation is another complicated subject in democratic government. The complication arose from what should be the criterion or basis of representation, an issue on which opinion is divided among scholars. Population, territorial and functional criteria are either used selectively, or in combinations. In Nigeria and USA both population and territorial criteria are employed in the elections to the two chambers of the National Assembly, and the Congress respectively. In the former Soviet Union, the functional criterion was added in the election to the 2,250 strong Congress of the People Deputies. On whether public officials should represent national or constituent interest, there is also no unanimity among scholars on whether public officials should represent the people's will or their interests, technically known as the mandate or independent theory of representation. While Thomas Hobbes and Alexander Hamilton preferred the reactionary theory, John Locke and Thomas Jefferson favored the Liberal theory and J. J Rousseau endorsed the radical theory of representation (Baradat 2000:139).

SELF-ASSESSMENT EXERCISE 1

Outline the difference between majority rule and proportional representation systems.

3.2   Pre-requisites for a good electoral system

The electoral system differs from one country to another. However, some features are common to all types of democratic systems regardless of their level of political development. Scholars have given conditions that can make an electoral system or election a worthy exercise. In Robert Darl's opinion, three conditions are essential to achieve a credible election. These are meaningful and extensive competition among individuals and organized groups for public positions; a highly inclusive level of political participation in the selection of leaders and policies, at least through regular, free and fair elections, such that no significant group of adults is excluded; civil and political liberties sufficient to ensure the integrity of political competition and participation.

In S. P. Huntington's view, an electoral system is democratic "to the extent that its most powerful collective decision makers are selected through periodic elections in which candidates freely compete for roles and in which virtually all the adult population is eligible to vote." To be able to achieve the conditions stipulated by these two scholars, most democratic states have put in place some electoral requirements. These include the division of a country into electoral districts known as constituencies. Population is the most common criterion used for the delimitation of the country into electoral units of roughly equal sizes, with each constituency being entitled to one representative in a single member constituency, or more than one representative in multi-member constituency.

Another is the registration of voters and its periodic revision especially before a major election. The exercise will ensure that every citizen who is eligible to vote on account of age, residential qualification, property educational or any other eligibility criteria is registered by the electoral body, and issued with a valid voter's card, without which he cannot exercise his franchise. The third essential element of an electoral system is the nomination of candidates for the election. In a democratic setting, candidates contest election on party's platforms. Members of a party who wish to contest usually go through either a convention or primary election where party members are delegates, or are handpicked by a select committee. There are however, rare cases when elections are conducted on a zero-party basis.

Political neutrality on the part of the authorities responsible for the conduct of elections is another pre-requisite for a sustainable democracy. The electoral umpire must be neutral and financially independent of other organs of government otherwise, electoral officials will always be suspected of manipulating the electoral process in favor of the incumbents. There must be level playing ground for all the contestants; the electoral boundaries should be delimited in such as way that no particular candidate or party should be favored; electoral materials should be evenly distributed across all the polling units and voters' list should be compiled and reviewed periodically to accommodate every citizen of voting age. Another requirement is that an electoral system should also ensure that parties and their candidates are given enough opportunities to articulate their positions on various issues at electioneering campaign. This is can also be done through mass media when all parties/candidates are expected to be given equal prime airtime, especially in government owned media houses.

Perhaps, the most important aspect of an election is voting itself. This is where voters express preference for parties or candidates of their choice. One man, one vote and secret balloting is the universally accepted standard practice in order to guarantee that voters cast their votes without any fear of intimidation. It is also important for counting, collation and declaration of election results to be done in the full glare of the public, and in the presence of accredited agents of the parties or candidates. Avenue for legal redress for a defected candidate should also be provided in an electoral law. Where a loser in an election has reasonable grounds to challenge a declared result, the instrumentality of an election tribunal is usually provided to enable him legal action to upturn results that, in his opinion, does not reflect the popular voters' will. It is also very important to dispose of election petitions within a reasonable time in order not to confer undue legitimacy to a winner, who may have manipulated the electoral process to his own advantage.

Power of recall is another feature of an electoral system in some countries, and it is applied sparingly, only in few cases when voters are convinced that it will be dangerous for the polity of retain, until the next election, the services of a representative who has been found to be unworthy of the people's mandate. There are stringent requirement before a constituency can invoke the power of recall. However, it was successfully applied in U.S.A's electoral history while in Nigeria; all attempts to apply in the past were stalled. But Harold Laski (1982:320) has warned of the danger of converting the power of recall to a weapon of "easy use" in order to prevent representatives living under the shadow of "a particularly ugly Sword of Damocles".

In summary, the electoral system has many implications for the political culture in any given country. Indeed it could be reasonably argued that the political culture to a large extent is a function of the electoral system. Therefore a political system will remain stable only when it has the broadest possible and legitimate basis for leadership recruitment and rejection, and majority of the citizens accept the electoral machinery as fair and just.

SELF-ASSESSMENT EXERCISE 2

Explain how the power of recall can become a 'Sword of Damocles in the hands of a political godfather.

3.3 History of the electoral in Nigeria

The history of elections in Nigeria began in 1923 following the promulgation of the Clifford's constitution of 1922; an electoral system was introduced to regulate the elections into three legislative seats in Lagos and one in Calabar. It was based on a restricted franchise of 100 pounds per annum. In 1946, no major change was made in the electoral requirements, except the reduction in income requirement to 50 pounds. The major landmark in the history of electioneering in Nigeria was the introduction of party politics by the Macpherson's constitution of 1951, which led to the evolution of the political parties that contested elections into the regional Assemblies. The parties were: The Action Group AG), led by Chief Obafemi Awolowo and was in control of the Western Region; The Northern Peoples' Congress (NPC), led by Sir Ahmadu Bello and was in control of the Northern Region while the National Convention of Nigerians and Cameroons (later National Convention of Nigerian Citizens) (NCNC), which controlled the Eastern Region. During the 1954 and 1959 regional elections in the

East and West, universal adult suffrage was used, but it was modified during the 1959 Federal elections when the East and West adopted universal adult suffrage, and only the North used male adult suffrage. The above is to show you that the history of electoral process and institutions, as well as their administration in Nigeria dated back to the colonial era. The first electoral institution established to manage the administration and conduct of elections in Nigeria was the Electoral Commission of Nigeria. The ECN administered and managed the conduct of the 1959 pre-independence general elections that heralded Nigeria's first republic.

In the First Republic the body was renamed the Federal Electoral Commission (FEC) by the administration of late Sir Abubakar Tafawa-Balewa. The Commission conducted the controversial General Elections of 1964 and the West Regional election of 1965. The manner the two elections were conducted and the crises they triggered combined to cause the collapse of the First Republic. In preparation for the 1979 elections, the General Olusegun Obasanjo's regime established the Federal Election Commission (FEDECO). The commission established in 1978 was disbanded in 1983 by the military because of its glaring partiality and culpability in the massively rigged 1983 elections, which returned then incumbent President Shehu Shagari to power in what was then described as "a land slide victory". This shoddy performance was in spite of the setting up of the Justice Ovie Whiskey Panel by the administration of Alhaji Shehu Shagari to probe into allegations of electoral fraud in the 1979 elections, and to make recommendations to guard against same in future elections. The consequence of the 1983 electoral debacle is that the military terminated the second term administration of Alhaji Shagari on December 31st 1983. Given its interpretation of the state of the nation and its leaders' disdain for politicians the Muhammadu Buhari's administration did not bother itself with a political transition program. However, on assumption of office on 27th August 1985, General Babangida committed his administration to a program of transition to civil rule. In 1987, following the report of the Political Bureau, he established the Electoral Commission (NEC) initially headed by Professor Eme Awa and later by Professor Humphrey Nwosu. The commission was charged with the responsibility of managing the electoral process during General Babangida's staggered and flamboyant transition process. Though NEC managed to conduct local, state and national assembly elections, the annulment of the presidential election in June 1993 called to question the integrity of the whole transition program. Though, Chief Abiola was denied his victory, but Professor Nwosu in a book published in 2008, fifteen years after the 1993 presidential election confirmed that Chief Abiola actually won the election, an information known, though unofficially, to most Nigerians.

The regime of General Sani Abacha in November 1993 succeeded the lame duck Interim National Government led by Chief Ernest Shonekan and established the National Electoral Commission of Nigeria (NECON). Abacha also preoccupied himself with an unpopular self-succession program, which alienated the vast majority of Nigerians, transformed the country into a pariah state and alienated her from the mainstream of civilized world community. After the demise of General Sani Abacha, his successor, General Abdusalami Abubakar overhauled the electoral commission, and renamed it the Independent National Electoral Commission (INEC). The commission came into being via the enactment of Decree No 17; of 1998 (now Act of Parliament). INEC's responsibility as contained in the Third Schedule of the 1999 constitution of Federal Republic of Nigeria is the conduct and management of the electoral process in the country.

INEC successfully conducted the series of elections, which ushered in the nation's Fourth Republic in 1999. The commission also conducted the second general elections of 2003, which did not go without criticisms. Predictably, in the conduct of the 2007 General Elections INEC seemed to have perfected the art and science of rigging. In 2003, what mattered was the disposition of election officials to the candidate. Indeed in 2003, the cliché "those who vote decide nothing but those who count decide everything" became a popular way for describing the farce in the electoral process. In 2007, the incumbent president described the election as a "do or die affair" and little wonder, the opposition parties were almost wiped off from the political scene when the results were announced. Almost three years after the 2007 General Elections were lost and won; the litigations arising there from have not been completely disposed of at election tribunals. This is not good enough for the survival of democracy.

What is obvious from the history of elections in Nigeria from the First Republic till date is that Nigeria politicians have not imbibed the appropriate political culture that will ensure a dispute and rancor-free electoral process, and in turn assure the stability of the polity. Both the government and opposition parties are guilty of electoral malfeasance. It is true that the factor of incumbency is potent everywhere including the established Western democracies. But in Nigeria, the incumbency factor has been extended to include public fund to finance the ruling party to the detriment of the opposition parties. Opposition parties are also prevented from having equal access to government-owned media outfits. In some cases, security agencies are used to intimidate opposition groups.

You need to note that a typical Nigerian politician has not imbibed the culture of accepting the result of an election even where has been squarely defeated in a free contest This is unlike the practice in advanced democracies where losers willingly accept defeat and immediately plan for the next election. In Nigeria, a clear loser not only engages himself in needless litigations but may also engage in subversive activities or openly call for a military coup. The reason is obvious. It is not in the character of a Nigerian politician to contemplate life outside government because of the power of patronage political power confers. Little wonder, he is always ready to put the rule of the game in abeyance, in pursuit of power at all costs.

Until recently in Nigeria, people seem to look forward unto a military intervention - an illegal and illegitimate government - as the only available option because people have lost faith in the ballot box as the only peaceful means of changing a bad government. Thus, this lends credence to the axiom: "those who make peaceful change impossible makes violent change inevitable. The consequence, as a retired Supreme Court in Nigeria, Justice Kayode Eso puts it is that, "military dictatorship rather than being a temporary expedient became the rule, civil rule, the exception, serving only as an interregnum to the military regnum"(Eso 2000;258). Experience has however shown worldwide that military regime is never an alternative to a democratic government. Writing on the Oliver Cromwellian's regime, Henry Hallam (cited in Williams, 1982:xviii) also wrote: "It is not in general difficult for an armed force to destroy a government but something else than the sword is required to create one. Therefore, it is only when an appropriate electoral system is put in place that the goal of an enduring political stability can be realized in any democratic system.

SELF-ASSESSMENT EXERCISE 3

List the reasons for electoral malpractices in Nigerian politics.

4.0   SUMMARY

In this unit, we have discussed the importance of the electoral system as one of the major requirements for a free and fair election. We also identified two types of electoral systems: the majority rule and proportional representations models and explained that each of them has its own merits and disadvantages. The unit also elaborated on the conditions that can ensure the conduct of a credible election in any democratic society. We finally took a trip on the history of the conduct of elections in the country and submitted that the record, so far, has been abysmally poor.

5.0   CONCLUSION

The ultimate of goal of the analysis we have carried out in this unit is not to paint a picture of gloom about the poor character of electoral competitions in Nigeria, or to go away with the impression that the Nigeria's case is hopeless. Rather, it is to attempt at finding appropriate solutions to the problems so identified. This is why a correct diagnosis of an ailment is always seen as a major pre-requisite to finding remedies since a wrong diagnosis is worse than no diagnosis at all. The idea of electoral reforms, which will be discussed in the next unit, is one major effort in this direction.

6.0   TUTOR-MARKED ASSIGNMENTS

1.   With sufficient reasons recommend the most appropriate electoral system that can stem the spate of electoral malpractices in Nigeria
2.   How can the system of proportional representation eliminate the draw backs or inadequacies inherent in the majority rule system? Assess the role of the Judiciary in the handling of election petitions in Nigeria during the 2003 and 2007 General Elections

UNIT 7 ELECTORAL REFORMS AND DEMOCRATIC SUSTAINANCE

1.0 INTRODUCTION

Due to the problems associated with the conduct of elections in Nigeria, governments, at different times, have taken steps to reform the electoral system, in order to ensure that the ends of democracy are met. The need for electoral reforms has been a recurring staple or element of the country's democratic process. This unit takes a general look at the subject of electoral reforms, examines the problems that have confronted the electoral process in Nigeria and makes a case for electoral reforms, using the Muhammed Uwais Panel's report as a reference point aimed at establishing the right conditions for sustainable democracy in Nigeria.

2.0 OBJECTIVES

At the end of this unit, you should be able to:

- explain the problems associated with the electoral process, particularly in developing countries
- analyse the importance of regular reforms of the electoral system as a major prerequisite for free and fair elections
- discuss the recommendations of the Justice Muhammed Uwais' Panel and what it portends for future elections in Nigeria if implemented.

3.0 MAIN CONTENT

3.1 The Imperatives of Electoral Reforms in Nigeria

The problems confronting elections and electoral process in the nation's democratic history can be linked to behavioral and attitudinal dispositions of the political elite (Almond; 2005). Part of the blame can also be placed at the door-step of institutions that have being saddled with the responsibilities for the conduct of the elections. Experiences have shown that rather than being independent of the executive and non-partisan, electoral commissions for the greater part of Nigeria's political history have been tied to the apron string of the incumbent executives. They not only lack independence and transparency in their dealings with politicians, and in the discharge of their functions, they are also far from being accountable and responsive to other stake- holders involved in the electoral process.

The history of election in Nigeria's efforts at democratization has not been an impressive one since independence. This is because electoral conduct in the nation political history has been marred by fraudulent practices, corruption and violence. It is therefore of little surprise that past efforts at democratization has collapsed at the altar of perverted elections and electoral process. So bad was the situation that elections period has come to be associated with violence and politically motivated crises. That politics has been converted into a money-making venture, has reinforced the notion of election as a contest that is meant to be won at whatever cost possible (Gboyega, 1977). This has turned electoral conduct in Nigeria to a war-like situation. From the electoral commission of Nigeria (ECRT) of the First Republic to the Independent National Electoral Commission (INEC), of today, electoral commissions in Nigeria have not demonstrated the detachment, including competence that are required in the discharge of their functions. Their inability to effectively manage the conduct and administration of elections and electoral process has consistently frustrated the nation's efforts aimed at instituting a credible and virile democratic system.

It is significant that on assumption of office President Musa Yar'Adua recognized the flawed nature of the election that brought him into office. He therefore promised to set up a panel to review the electoral laws in the country. On August 28, 2007 President Umar Musa Yar'Adua announced the setting up of electoral reform panel headed by the former Chief Justice of Nigeria, Muhammed Uwais. The Uwais' committee made far-reaching recommendations that bordered on constitutional amendments, institutional strengthening and value reorientation, including the granting of more autonomy to the Independent National Electoral Commission (TELL, January, 26 2009: 19-23).

The President later inaugurated a three-man panel headed by the Justice Minister, Chief Aondonka. The Aondoaka's panel tampered heavily with the recommendations of the Electoral Reform Committee (ERC). For example, it submitted that the appointment of Chairman of the

National Electoral Commission (INEC) should not be made by the President (Vanguard, December 12, 2008: 19). The government in its white paper, which was in line with Aondoaka's review, seriously tinkered with the Uwais' report, and came out with positions that were at variance with the aspirations of most Nigerians. The government's argument is that the involvement of the National Judicial Commission in the appointment of INEC chairman would violate the principle of Separation of Powers. The National Assembly however rejected a proposed bill from the Presidency, which sought to set up another commission that was to handle party registration. In the wise opinion of the lawmakers, that proposal was considered an unnecessary duplication of the functions of INEC and an unjustified waste of government resources.

Accomplishing far reaching electoral reforms for Nigeria is no doubt a major challenge that confronts the present administration in Nigeria. Obviously, in the 1999 General Elections there were allegations of electoral manipulations. However, the scale was not as massive as that of 2003 or unavailingly sweeping as that of the 2007. Worse still, the manner the re-run Governorship election in Ekiti state was conducted in April 2009 by INEC under Yar'Adua's watch shows that no lessons were learnt by the politicians, or remorse shown by the electoral umpire that had been severally indicted by the electoral tribunals, including the Supreme Court (Nurudeen, 2009: 301) . The continuous nullifications of election results in many states of the federations are confirmations that what passed for elections in 2007 and other re-runs since 2008, were, at best selections, or at worst, charades, in spite of INEC's verdicts. Only the recently conducted Governorship election in Anambra state on February 6th 2010 gives a ray of hope about future elections in Nigeria. There is no doubt, the reason for the choice of Ghana as the first African country to be visited in July 2009 by the United States' President; Barrack Obama was a subtle indictment of Nigeria's electoral process. According to the United States' "Ghana has now undergone a couple of successive election in which power was transferred peacefully, even in a very close election...President Mills has shown commitment to the rule of law' (Guardian, July 7, 2009: back page).

SELF-ASSESSMENT EXERCISE 1

Classify the problem of electoral malpractices as attitudinal or systemic challenges.

3.2   Uwais Electoral Reforms Committee'sRecommendations

In view of the far reaching recommendations of the Uwais' committee on electoral reforms, it is imperative that we examine in greater details the committee's understanding of Nigeria's electoral problems and how it proposes that they could be addressed. In carrying out its assignment, the committee reviewed the country's electoral history and established that "the lack of independence by the electoral commissions at both federal and state levels is a key deficiency of Nigeria's electoral process." In the committee's review of 85-year history of elections in Nigeria since 1922, it observed a "progressive degeneration' of outcomes with the 2007 election believed to be the worst.

The panel in its report affirms further that the major problem with the nation's electoral system is the lack of credible elections. The committee noted that the perceptions of the people about election are part of the critical elements that determine the success of electoral practices and regretted "the elections mind set of Nigerians as not only largely negative; they are also largely irrational". The committee's recommendations are therefore, aimed at achieving the desired positive mind set in the electorate so as to minimize violence and rigging in elections, including building lasting democratic institutions and cultures. Mohammad Uwais, a former Chief Justice of Nigeria, who headed the 22- member committee noted:

The committee is firmly convinced that the acceptance and implementation of the recommendations contained in this report will significantly restore confidence in the electoral process and usher in an era of free, fair and credible elections in the country. (Vanguard, Friday, December 12, 2008)Some of the committee's recommendations require changes in the existing electoral procedures, reallocation of electoral functions or creation of new institutions. Some of them require new legislations, while others require amendments of existing laws. Leaving nothing to chance to quickening the implementation process, the committee prepared draft of three bills: Act to Amend 1999 constitution; Act to Amend 2006 Electoral Act; and Act to establish Electoral Offences Commission.

Highlights of the Panel's Recommendations

3.2.1 A genuinely Independent INEC

The committee recommends that the Independence National Election Commission (INEC) should be massively re-organized and repositioned to ensure its independence and professionalism. It therefore recommends that the 1999 constitution be amended to ensure that INEC becomes truly independent, nonpartisan, impartial, professional, transparent and reliable as an institution and in the performance of its constitutional functions. For INEC to be truly independent, it is recommended that Section 84 of the 1999 Constitution be amended by adding subsection (8) to read: "The election expenditure of the independent electoral commissioners offices (addition to salaries and allowances of the chairman and members) shall be first charge on the Consolidated Revenue Fund of the Federation" (TELL, January 26, 2009).

The committee also recommends that INEC be split into two bodies: a board that formulates broad electoral policy and direction, and a professional/technical election management agency to handle the actual conduct of the elections. The INEC board shall be composed of 13 members as follows: a Chairman and deputy chairman who must not be the same gender; six persons representing the six geo-political zones of the country two of whom must be female; and five nominees representing the civil service organizations, labor organizations, the Nigerian Bar Association, NBA, women organizations and the media. Once appointed, a nominee cannot be recalled by any organization. The chairman and the deputy shall be persons of integrity, nonpartisan, possess vast professional/administrative/academic experience and must not be less than 50 years old. The other 11 members shall also have the same qualifications but must not be less than 40 years of age.

The nomination process, as suggested is to be no less rigorous. For the positions of chairman and the six geo-political zones, the National Justice Council NJC, shall advertise all the positions; receive applications/nominations from the general public and shortlist three persons for each position. These shall be forwarded to the National Council of State to select one and forward to the Senate for confirmation. For the other five members, each professional body shall forward three nominees to the NJC for screening, after which it shall make appropriate recommendations to the National Council of State, which would, after further screening, recommend one each to the Senate for confirmation. The tenure of office of the members shall be five years, subject to renewal for another five years.

3.2.2 Unbundling of INEC

One of the most radical, though contentious, reforms suggested is the unbundling of INEC. The committee stated that for INEC to function efficiently, some of the functions it presently performs should be assigned to other agencies. Consequently, it recommended the creation of three new agencies. These are: Political Parties Registration Council,

PPRC; the Electoral Offences Commission; and the Constituency Delimitation Commissions. The PPRC would, among other things, register political parties in accordance with the 2006 Electoral Act and monitor the organization and operation of the political parties, including their finances. It shall be made up of a chairman and deputy who must be of different gender and six national commissioners representing the six geo-political zones, two of whom must be women. The procedure of appointment and tenure are the same as that of the INEC board and the technical management team. Members can be removed by the President on the recommendation of the NJC (TELL. January 26, 2009).

A new autonomous and constitutionally recognized body called the Electoral Offences Commission has been recommended to be established through a bill of the National Assembly and empowered to perform functions, which include: investigation of all electoral frauds and offences; co-ordination, enforcement and prosecution of offences and the enforcement of the Electoral Act 2006, the constitutions of registered political parties and any other Acts or enactments. It shall be the chief executive officer; a deputy Chairman; six representatives of the six geopolitical zones; the Attorney- General of the federation or his nominee, not below the rank of an assistant Inspector-General; and a Secretary who shall be the head of administration. The Chairman and members shall be non-partisan and appointed by the President subject to the confirmation of the Senate.

The third agency is the Constituency Delimitation Commission. This would be established with institutional representation from INEC, the National Population Commission, the National Boundary Commission, office of the Surveyor-General of the federation, the National Bureau of Statistics and the National Identity Management Commission. A fourth body, Centre for Democratic Studies, CDS, is recommended to be established to undertake broad civic education for legislators, political offices holders, security agencies, politicians, political parties and the general public.

3.2.3c Scrapping of State INEC

The committee recommends that the State Independent Electoral Commissions, SIECs, should be reorganized and structured into INEC to form a single election management body for the country. At the state level, INEC will have 37 directors, one for each of the 36 states and the Federal Capital Territory (FCT), appointed by INEC and to trained and posted to states other than their states of origin. At the local government level, INEC shall employ 774 full-time electoral officers, after public advertisement, and post them outside their local government areas. At least one-third of the numbers shall be women.

Similarly, 8814 full-time career assistant electoral officers should be employed by INEC by the same process and posted within their wards. To give this a legal backing Section 153 of the 1999 Constitution, which lists INEC as a Federal Executive Body would be amended by deleting Sub-Section 1 (f). Consequently, INEC should be deleted anywhere it appears in Sections 153 to 158.

3.2.4 Voting Process

On the voting process and procedure, the committee recommends the gradual introduction of electronic machines in future elections after a period of limited testing and experimentation. In future elections, accreditation and voting are to take place within a defined period. Agents of political parties are to be given copies of results and they have the rights to demand a recount on the spot, should the need arise. All election results duly signed and copies given to the party agents, the Police and the State Security Service should be announced at the polling stations by the presiding officer. INEC is expected "swiftly and publicly" to display detailed results of the elections, including all polling station results and collated information on the number of voters, vote cast, invalid votes and others.

Emphasis is on the transparency of the result process to assure all stakeholders that the election is free, fair and credible. To enhance this, results broken down at polling stations should be provided at each superior level and the result should be more comprehensive in details. For the presidential election, INEC is to publish the results down to the lowest level prior to declare a winner to demonstrate that the results are accurate and within expectation. The committee says that this is very important because without vote analysis, at least at the state level, it would be impossible to determine if all constitutional requirements for the election have been met.

3.2.5 Party Agents

Unlike the present practice where party agents are accredited on elections day, the committee recommends that the accreditation be done 14 days to the election. However, fears have been expressed about this recommendation that such a long space may make it easier for a switch of the accredited agents, reveal the identities of the non-aligned ones and expose them to danger or business deals to rig the elections (TELL. January 26, 2009)

3.2.6 Independent Candidacy

A novel introduction is the recommendation for independent candidates. If accepted, some credible persons would be allowed to contest elections, provided they meet two conditions, in addition to the provisions of the 2006 Electoral Law. It shall be a constituency-backed nomination by verifiable signatures of 10 registered voters in each ward of the constituency and on the payment of a financial deposit which is refundable if the candidate scores up to 10 per cent of the valid votes cast in the constituency.

3.2.7 Funding of Political Parties

The committee recommends that the government should continue to fund political parties either directly or through INEC. This will however be based on the performance of parties at any election. Parties are also encouraged to raise funds through other means such as sale of forms to candidates, fund-raising, individual and corporate donations and through commercial activities. However, there are ceilings to how much an individual can donate to a political party as follows; President, N20 million; Governor, N15 million; Senate, N10 million; House of Representatives, N5 million; Chairman of local governments, N3 million and councilor, N500, 000. This is to check the influence of godfathers who buy over candidates through large donations for which they later demand even larger returns.

3.2.8 A Mixed-Electoral System

The committee recommends a mixed electoral system, which is a combination of the majority rule system or first-past-the-post system and modified proportional representation for legislative elections at the federal, state and local government levels, except the Senate. For the House of Representatives, in the existing 360 constituencies would be filled by the first-past-the-post system, while for the Senate the committee recommends a mixed electoral system for the 108 seats. This will be replicated at the state and local government levels.

3.2.9 Disposal of Electoral Petitions before Swearing-in

Another recommendation is the conclusion of election disputes before the swearing in of elected officials. Unlike now when election disputes could last as long as the judges please, a time limit of six months has been set for the resolution of all disputes arising from an election. In this regard, a maximum of four months would be spent at the tribunal stage, while the appeals resulting from the tribunal stage should take a maximum of two months. The election will, therefore, be conducted six months ahead of handing over (TELL, January 26, 2009)

3.2.10 Rejection of zero-sum politics

Furthermore, the committee rejects what it calls the zero-sum approach to politics, more popularly known as winner-takes-all. Henceforth, political parties that win at least 2.5 per cent of the National Assembly seats shall be qualified for cabinet appointments. It is the considered view of the committee that this would reduce tension in the polity and give all stakeholders a voice in the governance of the country. This will also discourage smaller parties and less electorally influential politicians to embrace the attitude of joining 'Any Government In Power' (AGIP).

SELF-ASSESSMENT EXERCISE 2

Explain the most important recommendations of the Muhammed Uwais' Panel on electoral reforms.

3.3   The Importance of Electoral Reforms

The importance of an efficient electoral system cannot be overemphasized in any democratic political system. A good electoral system delicately balances the politics of participation with the politics of representation and ultimately contributes to the building of a viable and sustainable political culture. The act of participation in the electoral process in a country not only vests legitimacy on the decision makers, it also makes the voters conscious that they are active and effective participants, though in an indirect sense, in the decision making process of their country. In a country where a good electoral system is in place voting becomes much more than a ritual or a mechanical function but an important instrument of citizen-participation in the selection of their leaders.

After almost five decades of political independence and the fourth attempt at democratic government, Nigeria cannot be described, yet as a stable political system. No country, including the advanced democracies has yet devised a perfect process of electoral administration. But the difference between those countries and most developing states, including Nigeria is that they have subjected their electoral procedure to an uninterrupted practice, and over the years their electoral systems have not only matured but have also endured. It is for this reason that an electoral reform becomes the most significant step towards realizing the goal of free and fair elections and sustainable democracy in the country A closer look at the Uwais Panel's report will reveal that it is a summary of the major problems confronting electoral administration in

Nigeria which, include lack of capacity and shoddy preparation by the electoral commission, inadequate logistics and irregular electoral outcomes that have severally been confirmed by the courts. While most of the election results have been upheld on ground of substantial compliance, this has not removed the odious stigma or lack of credibility or legitimacy on the beneficiaries of such controversial judicial decisions. Using the language of system analyst, these electoral related problems in Nigeria can be broadly categorized as system, process and policy inadequacies, and will continue to haunt the conduct of elections in the country unless they are addressed at their roots. But unfortunately, the attitude of the National Assembly towards electoral reforms in Nigeria conveys the impression that the laws makers are not enthusiastic about the reforms since according to Ume Ezeoke, the All Nigerian People's Party's (ANPP) National Chairman, the present political leadership in the country is loath, and apprehensive of any constitutional review, or electoral reform because as the major beneficiaries of the present unfair system, they are deliberately thwarting any move that may likely endanger their vested interests (Guardian, July 1, 2009:8). The legislators' attitude is a desire for self-preservation, and to expect them to proceed in the urgent manner that most Nigerians desire is to make them embark on an exercise in self-destruction or immolation.

The Peoples Democratic Party (PDP), the ruling party in the country, and with a comfortable majority in the two Houses of the National Assembly and its control of more than two thirds of the states in the federation, has been identified as the biggest culprit in the conspiracy to frustrate the implementation of the recommendations of the Uwais Panel's report. One would also expect President Yar'Adua, with his well publicized Seven-point Agenda, if he is willing, to use his clout as the leader of the ruling party, to push his party members, to act swiftly, without further delays in (re)commencing the process of amending the relevant sections of the constitution and the electoral laws. Apart from the Uwais's report, there are many sources where the government can get inputs on the right thing to do.

Only recently, on February, 23, 2010, the former U.S.'s Ambassador to Nigeria, Mr. Walter Carrington delivered a lecture titled "Electoral Reform, Good Governance and Democracy: Lessons for Nigeria" where he stated that "the enormous powers wielded by the Independent National Electoral Commission were responsible for the flawed electoral process in Nigeria since return to democracy in 1999". He

suggested that INEC should be a "mostly administrative body" to stem the controversy over elections in Nigeria (The Guardian, February, 24, 2010). With all these interventions, the federal government cannot claim not to have sufficient push that will make it take the much-needed urgent step to carry out the reform of the electoral system in the country. Any further delay, about a year before the next General Elections in 2011, may cast doubts on the prospects of conducting free and fair elections in the country in future.

SELF-ASSESSMENT EXERCISE 3

Give reasons for the delay by the National assembly in considering the report of the Uwais' panel on electoral reforms.

4.0   SUMMARY

We have established a case for electoral reforms in Nigeria where we examined the problems that have confronted elections in Nigeria in this unit and the previous one. We highlighted the major recommendations of the Muhammed Uwais' panel on electoral reforms and stressed why it is important for the present administration to address the issues raised in the report with dispatch. This, in our view, is the only way the government can convince Nigerians that it has the intention to conduct credible elections in the country in 2011 and afterwards.

5.0   CONCLUSION

A more transparent electoral process in Nigeria is the only step that can enhance the credibility of the electoral system and the legitimacy of government in Nigeria. A country where the electoral process is riddled with disputes and rancor will not only defeat the goal of achieving a sustainable democracy in Nigeria, it will also do a great deal of havoc to the country's image among the comity of nations. Rather than the current preoccupation with rebranding campaigns, or symbolic appearances as an observer nation at G8 meetings, a more determined effort to undertake the much-desired electoral reforms will do more to make Nigeria earn the respect of civilized nations of the world.

6.0   TUTOR-MARKED ASSIGNMENTS

1.   Discuss the significance of electoral reforms in Nigeria before the next General Elections.
2.   Evaluate the role of the National Assembly and the Presidency in the task of enacting a new electoral law for Nigeria.

3. Assess the role of the Civil Society groups and the Media in the current drive to bring about the reform of the electoral laws in Nigeria.

MODULE 4
THEORIES OF POLITICAL AND SOCIALCHANGE

Unit 1   Spectrum of Political Attitudes
Unit 2   Major Political Ideologies
Unit 3   Revolution and Social Change

UNIT 1   SPECTRUM OF POLITICAL ATTITUDES

1.0   Introduction
2.0   Objectives
3.0   Main Contents
     3.1   Political Change and Citizen's Attitudes
     3.2   Major points on the Political Spectrum
     3.3   Analysis of Attitudes towards certain Political Concepts
4.0   Summary
5.0   Conclusion
6.0   Tutor-Marked Assignments

1.0   INTRODUCTION

In this unit, we will discuss the spectrum of political attitude, and identify the reaction of occupant of each point on the spectrum to political change. We will identify the actors from the extreme left through the middle and towards the extreme right on the spectrum. We will also examine the extent to which each of them, for example, the radical or moderate prefer change and the factors that condition their attitude or reaction to political change.

2.0   OBJECTIVES

At the end of this unit, you should be able to:

- Explain what is known as the spectrum of political attitude.
- Describe each of the point on a political spectrum, like the Radical on the extreme left and the Conservative on the right.
- Estimate the factors that determine how each of them seek or react to change, as well the criteria to measure change like its direction or depth.

3.0   MAIN CONTENT

3.1   Political Change and Citizen's Attitudes

Any coherent explanation of political change is not complete without knowing the direction and the values inherent in change. The conventional approach is to arrange the terms, radical, liberal, moderate, conservative and reactionary along a continuum in order to gain a perspective or understanding of each of them. Citizens who occupy each point on the political spectrum have an attitude about whether a change is necessary or not in the existing state of affairs (the status quo), and if not, why, and if yes, how? It is their attitude to political change that will determine the policies they will support or oppose, as well as the course of action they will opt for. Political change is not only a complex subject but is also fundamental to any society. Four things are relevant to the understanding of political change.

The first is the direction, which the proposed change, will carry society. When progress is demanded, it could be a change that will endorse the policy, which has been existing or that which has not existed before. Is it progressive or retrogressive? Will it carry society forward or backward? The second is to determine the depth of a proposed change. Would the desired change amount to a major or minor adjustment in society? Would it modify or replace an institution that is fundamental to the society, as it now exist? The third aspect is the speed at which people want change. Here the more dissatisfied the people are with the status quo, the more impatient they are likely to be and therefore, the more rapidly they want to change. The last factor is the method by which it occurs. Is it peacefully or violently, legally or extra legally? Political change can be achieved illegally as it was attained in Russia in 1917 or China in 1949.

The movement along a political spectrum should be devoid of emotional or moral values. New changes may be positive or negative. Let us now consider these four items or criteria and their relation to attitude to political change as represented at different points on the political spectrum.

SELF-ASSESSMENT EXERCISE 1

Identify four criteria that can influence, and can be used to analyze the concept of political change.

3.2   Major points on the Political Spectrum

3.2.1 Radical

A radical is on the extreme left of the spectrum of political attitude, and can be therefore impatient with less than extreme proposals for changing it. Hence, all radicals favor an immediate and fundamental change in the society. In other words, all radicals favor revolutionary change. Although all radicals want immediate change at society's foundation, but a few of them (pacifists) completely reject violence as a means to achieve justice. Excellent examples of pacifists include Mahatma Gandhi (2008), the famed father of Indian independence, who successfully employed non-violent approach during Indian struggle for freedom from British colonial rule. Another is Mr. Martin Luther King Jnr., the late civil right leader in American who followed Gandhi's footsteps and was famous for his "I have a dream" speech. Ironically, both of them died violently in the hands of radical assassins, who preferred the extreme method than dialogue.

3.2.2 Liberal

Liberals are close to the status quo point on the continuum, a factor that makes them to be significantly less dissatisfied with existing state of affairs than the radicals. Indeed, the liberals support the basic features of society; but are quick to recognize weakness in the society and therefore are anxious to reform the system. One of the most fundamental differences between a radical and liberal is the attitude of each toward the law. Radicals are opposed to the political system that governs them, so they often see the law as one way in which those who dominate society maintain their control. Liberals, on the other hand, generally respects the concept of law.

Although, they may want to change certain specifics of it, they usually will not violate it instead, they try to change the law through legal procedures. John Locke and Jeremy Bentham fall under this category.

3.2.3 Moderate

Moderates are fundamentally satisfied with the society, although they agree that there is room for improvement and recognize several specific areas in need of modifications. However, they insist that changes in the system should be made gradually and that no change should be so extreme as to disrupt the society. Unlike the other positions on the political spectrum, there is no philosophical foundation for the moderates' category. The Aristotle's advice about seeking the "Golden mean" is often cited as justification by the moderates for their attitude.

Being moderate or taking a mild position about issues such as legalizing abortion or death penalty, it is difficult to take a moderate position. An example of a moderate position in Nigeria is the idea of "a little to the left and a little to the right" which military President, Ibrahim Babangida promoted as the manifestoes of the Social Democratic Party (SDP) and the National Republican Convention (NRC), when the two parties were registered by the National Electoral Commission (NEC) for participation in the politics of the aborted Third Republic in the country.

3.2.4 Conservative

Conservatives are the most supportive of the status quo, and therefore are reluctant to see it changed. Conservatives support the status quo not so much, because they like it but because they believe that it is the best that can be achieved now. Lacking confidence in society's ability to achieve improvements through bold policy initiatives, most conservatives support only very slow and superficial alterations of the system. The most cautious of them often resist and are even afraid of seemingly minor change. Then tend to see an intrinsic value in existing institutions, and are unwilling to tamper with them, claiming that to do so might seriously damage that which tradition has perfected.

As Edmund Burke, a leading Conservative argues: the well-governed society is one in which people knows their place. As he put it: "The rich, the able and the wellborn govern, while the people of lower social rank recognize their betters and willingly submit to their rule." Burke also believes no single generation has the ability to create abrupt changes that will improve society. In his views, by tinkering with institutions that have endured over the years' they will only succeed in destroying them. He also perceived civilization as a fragile thing, which may ruin society, if not protected from human folly (Baradat, 2000).

3.2.5 Reactionary

Of all the political attitudes, only the reactionaries propose retrogressive changes; that is a policy that would return society to a previous condition or even a former value system. For example, when the Shah of Iran was overthrown in 1979 the new government headed by Ayatollah Khomeini returned the country to the pre-Shah era. By definition, reactionaries reject notion of social progress as defined by people to their left, look backwards with pleasant nostalgia to the past, and previously held norms or values, which kept such society going.

Compare the attitudes of a Radical and Conservative to the concept of political change.

3.3   Analysis of attitude towards certain political concepts

Each of the individuals we have identified above respond differently to some specific issues of concern to human societies. These include, among others, issues like human rights and equality.

3.3.1 Human and Economic Rights

The left is inclined towards personal liberty especially as conceived in human rights. In other words, those whose political act may be regarded as leftist placed emphasis on the extension of human rightists. Rightist minded political attitudes put emphasis on economic or property rights. Indeed, right-wings political attitudes consider property right as an inalienable right. Political rights, they believe can be used to equalize property ownership; so claimed the rightist.

3.3.2 Rationalism

Right-wing political attitudes tend toward irrationalism. For example, conservative believed in the known, tried and tested methods and institutions of society. They do not usually accept that human being can make improvement upon existing conditions. The left, on the other hand, believes in human rationality and contends that Marxism is after all anchored on the scientific method, including the recognition of the capacity of man to change his conditions for the better. Since the leftist minded political attitudes rely on the application of human reasoning and intellects, we can say it is more consistent for man's quest for progress.

3.3.3 Nationalism

Rightist believed in Nationalism and metaphysical thinking. Leftist believed in internationalism, insisting that national frontiers are artificial and meant to promote exploitation in the name of national sovereignty, and non-interference in domestic affairs. The boundary leftists recognize is human and not geographical.

3.3.4 Equality

The left is equalitarian minded whilst the right is elitist. Leftist emphasize the basic equality of humanity. The left wing politician will argue that conditions for decent and equal living should be for everybody. The rightist will argue that society is stratified and that human beings are unevenly endowed. This thinking epitomizes elitism. The rightist will say that some people are innately superior to the other while the leftists will say that men have equal talent or latent ability, what those talents are they do not know unless they are developed. They argued further that when all talents have been developed, each must be given equal opportunities to contribute to social development. According to the leftist, if individual's talent is not developed, it is not the individual that suffers from it but the society as a whole.

Many people suspect that economic pressures are the primary motivating factors that determine the particular political position a citizen takes. Other factors include age, which makes the youth to be more liberal than the aged, educational status, psychological disposition, sex etc. Elderly people, unlike the youths have very limited time to live which make them to bother less about change, the impact of which they may not live long to enjoy. However, the youths are rightly described as the leaders of tomorrow and for that reason they usually view issue of change as that which their future. This makes the age structure of a country's population an important factor in political change making the youths the fuel and raw materials for change and the old people the major force that resist age.

Similarly, educational status is another factor that can make a citizen to either support or oppose political change. Those who are educated are able to properly evaluate the content of the proposed change, gauge the possible impact of method that is being planned to effect the change and the impact of such change on the fabric of society. In most societies, since the bulk of the property class is educated their attitude to change will certainly be influenced by the desire to preserve such interests. The uneducated do not possess the advantage of thoroughly weighing the merits and demerits of change, a factor that makes the probability that they plunge the society into change higher. In the same manner, the male are more prone to seek change than the female. The factors of physiology and maternity have combined to make women both physically and emotionally less prepared for the struggle that normally precede and accompany change, while men, on the other hand, are better endowed with those qualities of vigor and sacrifice which political change require.

SELF-ASSESSMENT EXERCISE 3

Discuss the role of Education and Age in making political change possible.

4.0   SUMMARY

In summary, our discussion in this unit centered on the major points on the political spectrum and their different attitude to change. For instance, while conservatives are averse to change, they support property rights, or private property. Liberals admit of non-harmful change and support human rights. Also while the radicals favor egalitarianism, the conservatives are opposed to change and are inclined to elitism. Conservatives are usually capitalist biased since the system tends.

5.0   CONCLUSION

Human beings by nature are afraid of change for the principal reason that they do not, or cannot know what the change portends for them. But experience has shown that what is permanent in life is change. Without the vision and commitment of those who believed in change, the world, probably, would not have witnessed the groundbreaking Industrial Revolution. We must recognize that most people for reasons of love of peace and stability prefer peaceful method of bringing about change. Yet, there are a few who out of dissatisfaction with the status quo are ready to stick their neck to effect change with whatever method that is available, or they can invent.

6.0   TUTOR-MARKED ASSIGNMENTS

1.   Analyse the importance of studying the spectrum of political attitude.
2.   Give reasons why personalities such as Mahatma Gandhi and Martin Luther King Jnr. are regarded as radicals with a difference.
3.   Explain the reasons why the Conservatives are often opposed to political change of any form.

UNIT 2   MAJOR POLITICAL IDEOLOGIES

1.0   INTRODUCTION

Ideologies are controversial, yet potent forces in academic discourse and the real world of politics. This Unit attempts a discussion of the major political ideologies that have dominated the world arena, especially after Adam Smith championed the course of capitalism in his classic, *The Wealth of Nations*. The unit continues with Karl Marx's treatment of evils of capitalism in *Das Capital* and how he along with Fredrick's Engels in the *Manifesto of the Communist Party* made a prediction of the proletarian revolution that will lead to the institution of a classless society. The Unit however goes beyond the doctrinaire or the polemics of the debates, but also employed recent and contemporary historical events/facts to either validate or rebut some of these, essentially, theoretical claims and postulations.

2.0   OBJECTIVES

At the end of this unit, you should be able to:

- define the concept of ideologies and the role they play in forming political attitudes
- explain the meaning and features of the major world ideologies such as capitalism, socialism and communism
- appraise these ideologies in such a way as to be able to recommend the most suitable or appropriate for your country.

3.0   MAIN CONTENT

3.1   Meaning and Definition of an Ideology

Ideologies were made necessary due to the challenges of the Age of Enlightenment when people believed they could improve their conditions by taking positive action instead of passively accepting life as it came. Prior to the modern era, people were discouraged from seeking solutions to their problems. Politics had not yet become democratized. Ordinary people were not allowed to participate in the political system. Politics was reserved for the kings heading a small ruling class. But this view changed with the democratization of politics, and the social and economic upheavals that accompanied the Industrial Revolution (Baradat 2000).

Political scientists do not agree on the exact definition of the term ideology. Frederick Watkins suggests that ideology comes almost entirely from the political extremes. Ideologies, he argues are always opposed to the status quo. They propose an abrupt change in the existing order; thus, they are usually militant, revolutionary and violent. In his view, most ideologies are stated in simplistic terms, utopian in their objective and usually display great faith in the potentiality of man for finding success and happiness. For example, the American Declaration of Independence, a political statement authored by Thomas Jefferson, and the Communist Manifesto, an economic doctrine, written by Karl Marx and Engels fall within this definition.

David Ingersoll suggests that each ideology includes assessments of the status quo and a view of the future.

Karl Marx argues that ideology is nothing more than a fabrication used by ruling class to justify their rule over the masses. Therefore, the dominant political ideas, or ideology of any society would always reflect the interests of the ruling classes, which according to him, were based on incorrect interpretation of the nature of politics. L.T Sarget argues, that ideologies are based on the value systems of various societies, and provides the believer with the picture of the world both as it is and as it should be.

Although these definitions differ in their emphasis, they all have enough in common to allow for broader understanding of the meaning of ideology. Ideology is primarily a political term, though it can be applied to other contexts. Second, ideology consists of a view of the present and a vision of the future. The preferred future is presented as a materialistic improvement over the present. This desirable future is often attainable, according to the ideology, within a single lifetime. As a result, one of the outstanding features of an ideology is its offer of hope. Third, ideology is action oriented. It not only describes reality and offers a better future, but most important, it gives specific directions, about steps that must be taken to achieve this goal. Fourth, ideology is directed at the masses (Baradat; 2000).

For example, Karl Marx, Benito Mussolini, Vladimir Lenin, Mao Zedong and Adolf Hitler directed their ideologies to the masses in their countries. In order to appeal to the masses, ideologies are usually couched in motivational forms. In a simple language, ideologies are the set of ideas from which the individual perceives himself; a set of ideas that lay down rules of correct behavior and provides a justification for the behaviour of the citizens; the purpose and ideals of society, the direction in which the nation is going and the norms and values to be upheld in changing circumstances within the life of the nations would be embraced in the national ideology. Having defined ideology from the eyes of different scholars, it is important we discuss some of the world influential ideologies.

SELF-ASSESSMENT EXERCISE 1

Explain the relevance of an ideology to a political system.

3.2   Capitalism

The rudiments of capitalism were developed from Adam Smith's notion of the "invisible hands" in his book, *The Wealth of Nations*, Smith (1776) advocated the principle of Laissez-Fare, which advocated that government should remain aloof of economic matters, but should rather allow the forces of demand and supply to direct the economy, thereby encouraging competition. Therefore, competition is regarded as the engine of the capitalist system because it rested on the assumption that "the good of the whole is best served when each person pursues his or her own self interest" (Baradat 2000:86). Capitalism can therefore be defined as an economic system under which the ownership of the means of production is concentrated in the hands of the minor section of the society. According to Awolowo (1978:57-61) capitalism has four basic concepts: private property, choice, equality and egoistic altruism. Only the fourth component requires elaboration since the other three are self-explanatory. Egoistic-altruism or what Smith called the 'invisible hands' suggest that while pursing his economic interest, every individual unconsciously promote at the same time the economic interest of others.

Historically, capitalism developed after the collapse of the feudal system. Its springboard was the Industrial Revolution in 18th century

England during which mechanization replaced human labor, which led to mass production of goods and services. Capitalism is also related to democracy since both emphasize freedom of choice and individualism, otherwise referred to as the survival of the fittest. Though capitalism originated in Europe, today the United States is regarded as the bastion of capitalism in the world. American capitalism reserves many of its greatest advantages with those with enough wealth to buy into the system. The adage "it takes money to make more money", and indeed to acquire political power, including the presidency, in US is true of American capitalist society.

However, the problem with capitalism is that it is exploitative and corruptive. Capitalism punishes abundance and rewards scarcity, labor is not rewarded in value commensurate to its input, the poor and the rich are left at the mercy of the few, who are rich. By means of monopolies or oligopolies, the capitalists are able to subvert the economy of any state in order to promote their self-interest and to injure the interest of the masses. Because the capitalist system eschews the idea of central planning it is always faced with intermittent crises, alternating between prosperity and recession. Capitalism also promotes fierce division between the upper class and the lower class in the society, thereby encouraging the law of the jungle among men.

However, beginning with the introduction of the welfare system in Europe, and the New Deal under President F. D. Roosevelt in US, attempts have been made to moderate the evils of capitalism. Nevertheless, since the collapse of the Soviet Union in 1991 and the discredit suffered by the socialist alternative because of this, and the apparent triumph of capitalism, Francis Fukuyama perhaps prematurely proclaimed "the end of history." He described the event as "the end point of mankind's ideological evolution and the universalization of western liberal democracy' (Huntington 1996: 31). Since then other countries such as Russia and China, in Asia and Tanzania and Nigeria in Africa have either joined the capitalist bandwagon or grafted free market principles into their system, thereby swelling the rank of the capitalist bloc, led by the United States, Japan, Germany and Britain.

SELF-ASSESSMENT EXERCISE 2

Identify major characteristics of a capitalist system.

3.3   Socialism

According to Karl Marx and Fredrick Engels, Socialism is an intermediate stage between capitalism and communism. Socialism is not only an economic system, but a movement and a complex ideology embracing social, political, and moral philosophy. Socialism has three basic features: public ownership of the means of production, distribution and finance, the establishment of a welfare state and a socialist intent. Socialism seeks to extend its activities to all undertakings with the objective of promoting equality and social welfare. It desires expansion of state activities not for personal gain but to assure freedom and justice to the individual. In order to achieve this lofty goal, planning is central to socialism. The traditional way to socialize an economy is by nationalization. Nevertheless, because of the problems associated with nationalization, socialists are wary of adopting this measure. Another problem with nationalism is that it has been discovered that some industries are best run and most productive when left with the private sector.

Apart from production, another equally important relevant issue to a socialist society is the distribution of goods and service. The introduction of the New Deal in the 1930s in by President Delano Roosevelt of USA despite being a capitalist state was one major attempt to even out the distribution of wealth in favor of the poor. However, unlike communism, socialism is not completely egalitarian; it merely attempts to narrow the gap between the haves and have-nots. While it recognizes individual differences, which account for differences in status, Socialism seeks to eliminate poverty and to assure reasonable and comfortable life for the citizens. The motto of socialism is "from each according to his ability and to each according to his deed."

The principle of socialist intent set the goal of making the citizens free from material dependence. Since the condition of scarcity under capitalism makes people to compete acutely, under socialism co-operation is expected to replace competition. The replacement of competition with co-operation in the machine age after the Industrial Revolution, the theory posits will lead to greater productivity, and disappearance of class differences, as well as the elimination of tensions within the society. In some respects, one can say that socialism is also compatible with democracy, since it is to the individual economically what democracy is to the individual politically. Socialism is therefore the economic equivalent of democracy.

According to Harold Laski, "Socialism is the logical conclusion of democracy" (cited in Baradat, 2000:191). It is well known that money is a major source of political power. Thus, J. J Rousseau argued that an economic system that distributes wealth more evenly would enhance the practice of democracy.

The major problem with socialism is that it has many variants. There is the scientific socialism, which strictly followed the doctrinaire exposition of Marx and Engels. The difference in interpretation, and the alleged shift from the original socialist dogma in the practice of the ideology in the former Soviet Union and China was one reason for the historic Sino-Soviet rift in 1950s. The Utopian socialism of Saint Simon and Robert Owen is also different from the Marxian approach because it sought to achieve socialist end through peaceful means. In the early days of African independence, some African leaders, notably, President Nyerere of Tanzania and, and President Kaunda of Zambia toyed with the idea of African socialism, which they called Ujaama and Humanism respectively. In Nigeria, Chief Awolowo equally advocated Democratic Socialism. Because of this lack of unanimity of view about socialism as an ideology, it is not unusual to hear people say: not all socialist are Marxists, but all Marxists are socialists. Before 1991, socialist countries in the world included many countries such as East Germany, Romania, Bulgaria and Poland, largely, if not mainly in Eastern Europe.

SELF-ASSESSMENT EXERCISE 3

Identify the differences between a capitalist and a socialist system

3.4   Communism

Communism is a social and political system based on the doctrine developed by Karl Marx and Fredrick Engels in their book *The Communist Manifesto* written in 1848. Communism interprets history, as a relentless war between the wealthy, and those who have work to earn a living. It teaches that the economy is the foundations of societies while others: politics, religion etc, which they called the superstructure, are determined by economic factor. The deep-seated conflict of interests between these two groups, they theorized, will lead to a class war between the oppressor and the oppressed class. In the end, the proletariat (the lower class) will emerge victorious, establish their hegemony and create a true socialist commonwealth. The communist reason that since history has shown that those who control power use it to perpetuate their dynasty, the democratic Utopia envisaged can only be attained through revolutionary or violent means (Azikwe, 1979: 26). As a first step, a dictatorship of the proletariat will be installed to eliminate all differences before the state apparatus will disappear.

Under capitalism, the state is an instrument of arbitrary coercion and oppression and its executive "is but a committee for managing the affairs of the bourgeoisie"- in their ruthless exploitation of the working class. As the dictatorship directs the society towards the building of an egalitarian society, there will be more willingness of every man to work to his own capacity since the fruits of labor will be shared more equitably. As the state apparatus withers away, the communist slogan then becomes "from each according to his ability and to each according to his need". However, contrary to the Marxian prediction, the Soviet Union, a non-capitalist country experienced socialist revolution in 1917. And for more than seven decades, until 1991, the Soviet Union remained a socialist state. Yet, it could be argued that Soviet experience did not approximate to genuine communism since the state structure did not "wither away" or disappear as predicted by Marx.

The reason for this is that Soviet Union never attained communism-the last and final stage of societal development. This was confirmed in 1961 when the Russian Communist Party declared that only socialism has been achieved, and in line with the view of the communist historian, Isaac Deutscher, the Bolshevik Revolution of 1917 was the beginning of the journey to communism (Watson 1993: 184). Under communism, the nation state system is distrusted because it developed along with capitalism. Marx argued that nation-states were organized by capitalists to create artificial separation from people who have a great deal in common, since according to him "working men have no country." The socialists Internationalists predicted that as various countries adopt socialism or communism, the need to break the artificial barriers among states would be realized.

A major feature of communism is the dominance of a one party organization. The communist party in Soviet Union before 1991, for example, had a long tradition of obedience to decisions once made by the party's hierarchy; while arguments could only be made about the interpretation of Marxism-Leninism, not about alternative to it. This arrangement complements the centrality of economic planning in such a way that nothing important is left to private enterprise. Communism also demand a strong bureaucracy and a considerable curtailment of freedom until the emergence of Mikhail Gorbachev in 1985 who introduced the ideas of *"Glasnost"* and *"Perestroika"* to reform the practice of communism in the old Soviet Union, and which ultimately led to the collapse of the Soviet-communist state and the abandonment of the ideology.

Since the collapse of Soviet Union, there have been attempts to discredit socialism and communism as alternative ideologies to capitalism. Though it is true that since the end of the Cold War, the socialist bloc has been in disarray, it is not conclusive that socialism has lost all its attractions, or is dead theoretically or politically. Presently, Cuba a Latin American country still believes in superiority of the socialist alternative, in spite of the determination of successive U.S.'s administrations since 1959, to undermine the Fidel (now Rao) Castro led government.

Differentiate between Socialism and Communism.

3.5   An Appraisal of different Ideologies

Having explained the meaning and features of the three main ideologies, it is important that we appraise these ideologies in order to have an idea which of them is the most appropriate for adoption today in the world, or in your country. First, an ideology suitable for a country is the type that its prescriptions have relevance for the peoples' political, economic, legal and educational systems, as well as their social relations. For a post-colonial state like Nigeria, an ideology that will shake off the imperial vestiges inherent in the country's educational system in such a way that its colonial orientation will give way to a development focused system.

An ideology that will wean the nation's legal system from its colonial orientation, in such a way that it is no longer a rehash of English Common Law, but a body of laws reformed in consonance with national values and mores, including the substitution of archaic notion of capital punishment, with a more equitable, just and fair system which is aimed at correcting rather than punishing offenders. An ideology that will create an economic climate conducive to increase capacity utilization and human resources development, as well as bridge the gap between the very many, who are poor, and the very few, who are rich.

The experience of former Soviet Union, and the persistence of the contradictions within her socialist system, is a pointer to the fact that a wholesale technical embrace of an ideology alone is insufficient as a national panacea. We now know that contrary to Karl Max's theoretical predictions, socialism did not lead to the withering away of the State. Mikhail Gorbachev's resort to *"Perestroika"* and *"Glasnost"* was not only an act of desperation but also an open admission that the Soviet system was overdue for reforms. Yet the reforms, novel as it was for an already atrophied system could not stop communism from being taken for a capitalist shock therapy, until it was abandoned by the Soviets.

Like socialism or communism, and in spite of the outward veneer of resilience, capitalism has also not succeeded to overcome its inherent contradictions. What has kept it afloat, and safeguarded it from collapse, is the adoption by most capitalist countries of what Karl Popper in his book *The Poverty of Historicism* has termed "reformist measures." This package is embodied in what is popularly known as welfare policies, such as unemployment benefits, old age-pensions, and state – sponsored

Medicare prevalent in capitalist Western European Countries. It alsopredates what Dr. Nnamdi Azikwe (1979) in his book *Ideology for Nigeria* christened Neo-Welfarism (Azikiwe 1977).

If we contrast Azikiwe's "Neo-Welfarism" to Awolowo's preference for "Democratic Socialism", or Nkrumah's "Scientific Socialism" or Nyerere's "Ujaama", it will, therefore, become clear that any discourse on ideology, is a pure academic or polemical exercise in dialectical dissent. We are not saying that ideology is not relevant simply because it is loaded with doctrinaire complications; but a more reasonable attitude is to embrace it with caution. Even before Karl Marx, the utopians Socialists such as Robert Owens and Saints Simon were divided. Joseph Proudhon, for instance, wrote *Philosophy of Poverty,* but Marx in bitter satiric reply wrote his famous *Poverty of Philosophy*. Yet both of them were espousing socialist thought. Karl popper's Open Society and The Poverty of Historicism is perhaps until date, the most devastating assault on Marxism and the theory of dialectics.

While the facts of a given event can be objectively determined and agreed upon by all reasonable people, but where ideology comes in, the interpretation of these facts are influenced by subjective factors, personal beliefs and value judgments. If this is the case, the search for an appropriate ideology for any country should go beyond adopting or rejecting a particular ideology. A suitable ideology, therefore, must be deliberately conceived, and the citizens must be psychologically nurtured to accept and embrace it. In a multi-national country like Nigeria, the reconciliation of the primordial goals of the disparate groups, which make up the country, within the context of an overarching national framework must be the focus of an ideology.

The need for this harmonization of goals and interests become more imperative if we realize that the former imperial powers that brought these groups together, motivated by the expediency of colonial interest, adopted the policy of "Divide and Rule", which tore these groups apart, rather than unite them. Azikiwe (1979:111-9) provided insight into how integration of these ideologies can be done through what he called an eclectic philosophy and the pragmatic approach. This is the only way avisionary leadership; supported by articulate citizenry can make a country attain the goals of socio-economic development and political stability, and not a strait jacket adoption of a national ideology.

SELF-ASSESSMENT EXERCISE 5

Estimate the justifications for the most suitable ideology for your country.

4.0   SUMMARY

In this Unit, we have examined the origins as well as the meaning of ideology as a political and philosophical concept. We also discussed the major ideologies and how the world has evolved from one ideology to the other. We noted that Karl Marx employed the principles of dialectics as well as economic determination, or the materialist conception of history to explain the inexorable forces and the motive that have been bringing about these changes. We, however, observed that the Bolshevik Revolution that occurred in 1917 did not technically follow Marx's prediction since Russia was not yet a capitalist state and the event did not lead to the withering away of the state. We ended the discussion by appraising the age-long debates between the supporters of the "status quo" and advocates of a utopian world.

5.0   CONCLUSION

Even before the advent of Marxist thought, any discussion about ideologies has always been a controversial topic. Indeed, until it received its own bouts of criticisms from the radical Marxian ideology, capitalism, in its early days when compared with feudalism was also revolutionary in its impacts. For this reason, most debates on ideologies are often polemical; between the defenders of an existing order, and those who seek the overthrow of that order, and its replacement with a new social order, which in the view of such proponents is considered more just, equitable and egalitarian. However, with the end of the ideological rivalry in 1991 following the collapse of the Soviet Union this disputation over the appropriateness of one ideology or the other has receded. In spite of the discredit that the socialist/communist ideology has received from the scholars who believe in "the end of history thesis", which has made many more countries in the world to embrace the freewheeling capitalist path, there are still a few doctrinaire or dogmatic Marxists who still hold tenaciously to the comparative efficacy of communism.

6.0   TUTOR-MARKED ASSIGNMENTS

1.   Describe the role do you think an ideology plays in mass mobilization in any country
2.   Explain the circumstances that contributed to the failure of the socialist/communist ideology in the former Soviet Union
3.   Account for the relative triumph or success of the capitalist over the   socialist ideology in the world today.

UNIT 3   REVOLUTION AND SOCIAL CHANGE

1.0   Introduction
2.0   Objectives
3.0   Main Contents
    3.1   Definition and Origins of Revolutionary Movements
    3.2   The 1917 Russian Revolution
    3.3   The 1949 Chinese Revolution
    3.4   The Cuban Revolution
    3.5   The African Revolution
4.0   Summary
5.0   Conclusion
6.0   Tutor-Marked Assignments

1.0   INTRODUCTION

A revolution is an unusual change of a state of affairs. It is different from an evolution, which is often a gradual, and a stage-by-stage means of adjusting or moderating a *status quo*. This unit takes a global and holistic view of the concept and process of revolution and social change. After defining the concepts, the unit also examines the techniques employed by revolutionaries to achieve their objectives. The unit also takes a historic excursion into different types of revolutions in the world, from the Puritan revolt in Britain, the American war of Independence and the French Revolution as preludes to the more ideologically based Marxist's conception of revolution.

2.0   OBJECTIVES

At the end of this unit, you should be able to:

- explain the meaning and the origins of the concepts of revolution and social change
- discuss the Unorthodox character of a revolutionary movement especially in the method it employs to achieve its objectives
- explain the differences in the nature of revolutionary movements from one country to another.

3.0   MAIN CONTENT

3.1   Definition and Origins of Revolutionary Movements

A revolution is a sudden or abrupt change in the social structure of a society. The concept of a revolution is distinct from evolution. While evolution is a gradual stage-by-stage progression, transition or development from one level to another, revolution is an unusual and often an un-orthodox means of effecting change. In the liberal social science disciplines there is the preference for the non-violent method of change, which made Claude Ake(1988) to describe "Social Science as imperialism". What Karl Marx and other succeeding generation of radical scholars such as Claude Ake, Ola Oni, Bade Onimode, Edwin Madunagu and Okwudiba Nnoli did was to transform the foot-dragging of bourgeois scholarship to open resistance of the critical school. They all conceive a revolution as political in character: it is concerned with the calculated overthrow of an existing political order, using as much force and terror as are deemed necessary to effect radical changes in men's moral, economic, social and intellectual lives (Nisbet, 1973:207). But for a revolution to succeed it also require two other pre requisites: religious zeal or mentality, in addition to military tactics. Indeed, without the religious, almost messianic preoccupation, the Jacobins would not have succeeded in carrying out the French Revolution. Similarly, V. I. was also clear about *What is to be Done?* In his *"The State and Revolution"* before he led the Bolshevik Revolution in Russia in 1917. Indeed, the resemblance between the words militant and military as weapons of revolution is more than verbal. But a revolution never occurs unless the objective conditions are ripe which makes violent change inevitable. These conditions include poverty, political deprivation or exclusion and social injustice. Lack of access to basic human needs are prime causes of revolutions, especially when poor people see others living much better. Most revolutionary movements therefore espouse egalitarian ideas, a more equitable distribution of wealth and power to appeal and awaken the consciousness in the masses.

Former President John Kennedy once explains one condition that contributes to a revolution, when he said: "those who make peaceful change impossible makes violent change inevitable". Contrary to popular impression, a revolution is not necessarily spontaneous; it has to be planned and be led for it to be meaningful and enduring. As Nisbet explained:

...The heart of every revolution, successful or unsuccessful lies in small minorities-elites as they are known in modern social theory-composed of dedicated, often professional trained individuals, conscious of themselves as communities, and working with technical knowledge as well as moral zeal toward the overthrow of a political order by whatever means are necessary.

Based on the criteria identified above, it is not easy to precisely place or date in history the beginning of the revolutionary tradition. There are those who believed that the American War of Independence in 1776 marked the onset of revolutionary movement or struggle. Others however argue that in the strict sense of the word, it was not a revolution but a war of liberation from the mother country, since the objective was limited and did not involve a total reconstruction of the fabric of the society. Others are also willing to turn backwards to the Puritan revolt of 1688 in which Cromwell, a soldier, played a vital role, and when after a civil war; the Parliament triumphed in a decisive victory over a now weakened monarchy. But unlike in the French Revolution where the unifying myth was earthly or worldly, the underlying pull and push in the Puritan revolt was eternal, Christian conviction, of the Jesuit order, championed by Ignatius Loyola, himself a retired soldier.

This makes the 1789 French Revolution that marked the end of the period of Royal absolutism of Louis XV the first ideal revolution in modern history because it fully satisfied these criteria. In spite of these different views, what is beyond debate is that each of these struggles represents a rejection or repudiation of the past and a fervent and determined desire for a new order. What is striking in 1776, and perhaps similar to other revolts in sentiments, is that the Americans not only wanted freedom from British rule they also embraced, as it was then, a novel and unprecedented republican democracy. In 1789, the French proclaimed freedom, equality and fraternity-a three-word slogan-employed by the coalition of the common people (The Third Estate) and the nobles (The Second Estate) to embark on the siege of Bastille, where the king (First Estate) held sway.

A similar victory was achieved in 1688 in what later came to be referred to as the Glorious Revolution, when the English rose up against the Catholic tyranny and James II fled to France. Another common theme in these three incidents is that those who desired change were already dissatisfied with the peaceful or conventional method; rather they were prepared for unorthodox means and actually, in all the cases, used violence or force to achieve their related objectives. Indeed, by opting for violence they clearly anticipated Karl Marx who in 1848 along with his life-long collaborator, Fredrick Engels later developed a more profound, brilliantly articulated and scientifically based violent method of reconstructing a new social order.

Examples of revolution in other countries of the world include: Russia 1917, China 1949, Cuba 1959, Algeria 1962, South Vietnam 1975, Cambodia 1975, Angola 1975, Iran 1979, Nicaragua 1979, Afghanistan 1992 and the Orange Revolution in Ukraine in 2004. But we will however discuss a few of them, citing two examples in Europe, one each in Asia and Latin America, including some countries in Africa where popular uprisings or revolts that are commonly referred to as revolutions have occurred.

SELF-ASSESSMENT EXERCISE 1

Account for the criteria that will qualify a popular revolt as a revolutionary movement.

3.2   The 1917 Russian Revolution

Vladmir I. Lenin was in exile in Siberia in the year 1898 where he encountered and studied the work of Karl Marx. He was released in 1900 and went to Switzerland where he turned into an apostle of Marxism. He later became part of the leader of the Russian Marxist movement. This movement split into two due to irreconcilable ideological differences over the interpretation and practical application of Marxism. The first group, the Mensheviks was led by the father of Russian Marxism Georgie Plekalov, they were the orthodox Marxists. They insisted that the dialectics had to run its full course before the proletarian revolution. As far they were concerned, Russia was not ripe for a revolution because it was still a feudal society in the pre 1917 years. They believed that without attaining the capitalist stage, a revolution in the Marxian sense was not possible.

On the other hand, the Bolsheviks, led by V. I. Lenin rejected the Menshevik theory as too dogmatic. They argued that under certain circumstances, the proletariat and the peasantries could join forces and take control of the state. Unlike Marx who spent a lot of his time analyzing capitalism and paying little attention to the socialist/communist utopian, Lenin was more pragmatic. Consequently, Lenin devoted himself to developing revolutionary doctrine and applying Marxism to a real situation. Lenin therefore restored violence to the doctrine, amended the theory to make it apply to under developed states and filled in the blank space that Marx had left regarding post-revolution proletarian society.

3.2.1 Ways by which V.I. Lenin modified the Marxist theory

1.   Violence is the only action that would bring about meaningful change.
2.   V. I. Lenin believed that the proletariat would not develop class-consciousness without the intervention of a revolutionary group. Someone must ignite the revolution; Lenin recommended not even the labor union because they could be bought over.
3.   Lenin believed that socialism could be imposed by a minority - a revolutionary vanguard - small, discipline, totally, dedicated group which must include total commitment.

4.   The vanguard of the proletariat in Russia was the Bolshevik party. It was renamed the Communist Party in 1918. The party would carry out the revolt or revolution and then impose a dictatorship on the entire society. As Lenin saw it, it was not to be a dictatorship of the Bolshevik over proletariat.

5.   Lenin also created a structure for the vanguard of the proletariat and the international movement. He called it the International Communist Movement; (the Committers). Its duty was to encourage socialist revolution would last or endure if other European nations embraced the socialist option.

6.   Lenin succeeded in October 1917 when the Bolshevik party carried out the socialist revolution in Russia. The revolution eventually led to the formation of USSR led first by Lenin himself, who later died in 1924.

Having laid the foundation of the socialist revolution in USSR, the mantle fell on his successor, Joseph Stalin who also died in 1956. From 1956 Nikita Khrushchev ruled for eight years until he was dismissed in1964. Leon Brezhnev took over and ruled until his death in 1982. A succession of aged leaders from Andropov to Chenecko ruled until 1985 when Mikhail Gorbachev, a relatively young leader emerged on the scene. He reasoned that the 1917 revolution had not really achieved its objectives, given the stagnation of the Soviet economy that had atrophied. Gorbachev therefore introduced far reaching reforms which altered the course of the socialist revolution in Soviet Union and ultimately to the disintegration of the Soviet Empire.

SELF-ASSESSMENT EXERCISE 2

Explain the methods used by V. I. Lenin to actucalise Karl Marx's revolutionary doctrine in Russia in 1917.

3.3   The 1949 Chinese Revolution

The Communist Party of China was founded in the year 1921. Mao Tse-Tung, the leader of the revolution was born in 1893 and later became the communist leader in China. The Soviet Union was interested in China and therefore, V. I. Lenin used the Committers to co-ordinate the efforts of the Communists in China. Mao wrote a book titled *Report on the Human Peasant Movement,* which called upon the Communists to abandon the cities for the countryside because the peasants not the proletariat were China's true revolutionaries. With this document, Mao led the formation of what became 'Maoist thought'. But it was not easy for Mao to get his thought translated into reality. The Nationalists led the government of China. There was a rivalry between the Nationalists and the Communists because the Nationalists were already in control in

China and they saw Mao's idea as a threat to their positions. The nationalists therefore decided to silence the communists. To avoid destruction or annihilation, the communists embarked on a Long March. It lasted a few years. About 100,000 people embarked on that journey which covers 6,000 miles, only 35,000 survived (Baradat, 2000). A new base was established in Shensi province where the March ended. In 1949, Mao led the peasants to successfully overthrow the Nationalists' government in a revolution.

3.3.1 Principles of Maoism

First, when the Communist Party in China took control of government it introduced the five year plan which attacked the absentee's land lords, sought to socialize the economy and also made it to be collectively owned. Second, Mao allowed the people to criticize his government unlike the Soviet method of suppressing dissent and imposing conformity or uniformity on the people. To achieve this Mao used the phrase: "let a hundred flowers bloom, let a hundred schools contend." Third, Mao believed in the idea of permanent revolution because it is the only means by which people can achieve their goals. Mao did not believe in institutionalization or bureaucratization but in mass movement.

Fourth, Mao rejected Lenin's elitist reliance on the party to lead the revolution. Mao therefore, invoked the slogan "red over expert" and called for the mobilization of the masses, which he called the last line of defense of the revolution.

Fifth, Mao believed in guerilla warfare. Unlike Marx who believed that revolution would happen by itself or Lenin who spoke of a vanguard party to telescope a revolution. Mao believed that revolution would happen over a long period. Sixth, Mao identified two objectives of a revolution: military and political, the two being inseparable, since as he puts it "political power also flows from the barrel of the gun". According to him, the first military goal of a guerilla war is to preserve oneself and destroy the enemy. And this can be done by destroying the fighting capabilities of the opponent. The only thing essential to the guerilla is the safe zone. Politically, war is not won until you have convinced your opponent about the rightness of your course. As Mao put it, "surround the cities with the country side".

Mao said in 1949 when he led the revolution: "From today on, the Chinese people have stood up. Never again will foreigners be able to tramp us."

SELF-ASSESSMENT EXERCISE 3

Identify the major behind Mao's type of revolution

3.4   The 1959 Cuban Revolution

Fidel Castro was born in 1927. His country, Cuba was under a dictator, named Fuldencio Batista. In 1953, Castro tried to seize a military installation but failed. He was arrested and imprisoned but was later released in 1955. Castro went into exile in Mexico and returned to Cuba in 1956. He built a large following of supporters among the peasantry to whom he promised land reforms and redistribution. Just like Mao, he embarked on guerilla warfare, which eventually toppled or overthrew the government of Batista in December 1959. Since assumption of office in 1959, the communist inspired government of Fidel Castro faced consistent United States' hostility, which reached its peak in 1961 when the John Kennedy's administration sponsored the Bay of Pig insurrection against Castrol's government.

However, with the support of the Soviet Union Castrol was able to ward off this rebellion, including the international outrage and anxiety generated over the Cuban Missile Crisis, a dispute that pitched Washington against Moscow. American consistent grouse against Cuba included Castrol's anti imperialist postures, description of U. S. as the colossus of the North, and his determination to export or ignite revolution in other Latin American countries, including African states, notably, Angola. Despite U S's opposition, Cuba has remained a communist state in the Americas like an oasis in a desert, and Castrol retained his position first as Prime Minister, until 1976 when he took the title of President. Due to ill-health, he yielded his office to his brother, Rao, in 2008. Though still a third world country the 1959 revolution has recorded modest achievements for Cuba in the fields of education, public health and racial equality, including substantial investment in the area of agriculture, especially sugar-cane production, its major foreign exchange earner.

SELF-ASSESSMENT EXERCISE 4

Assess Fidel Castrol's government in line with the objectives of the 1959 revolution in Cuba.

3.5   Revolution in Third World/African countries

Most third world and African countries have had revolutionary movements at some times before and since their independence. During the cold war years, the typical third world revolutionary movement was a communist insurgency based in the countryside. Those who view their leaders as promoting what they called US imperialism, which they consider to be against their national interest, organize such revolutions. Consequently, the domestic politics of third world countries were coloured by the great power politics in the East-West contest. In reality, many of these governments and revolutions had little to do with global communism, capitalism or imperialism. They were indeed local power struggle largely between rural ethnic groups into which great powers, for selfish reasons, were drawn.

The end of the Cold War in 1989 removed super power support from both sides of domestic politics; and the collapse of the Soviet Union in 1991, and the adoption of capitalist oriented economic reforms in many countries, including Russia and China, reduced the appeal of communist directed revolution. Although third world revolutions usually advocate for the poor versus rich, nationalism versus imperialism, the particular character of these movements varies across regions. In the Arab world, for instance some of the most potent revolutionary movements are motivated by extreme, or in the Western usage, fundamentalist interpretation of Islamic doctrine as it was successfully launched in Iran in 1979 and Afghanistan in 1982. Islamic political activities in the Middle East derive their main base of strength from championing the cause of the Palestinians against Israel (Zionism), or against the idea of exclusive nuclear club or selective proliferation, or the poor masses against the rich elites. Thus, radical group like the Hezbollah runs school, hospitals, and control 12 seats in Lebanon's parliament as at 2001 (Goldstein). Through such activities, they gain legitimacy in the eyes of their people, rather than being perceived as terrorist organizations.

In Africa also, where colonialism led to the creation of artificial boundaries that were at variance with ethnic divisions, many revolutionary claims or movements have continued to have a strong tribal appeal or primordial base, as it was successfully demonstrated in the secession of Eritrea from Ethiopia, and is ongoing in countries such as Sudan and Cote de Voire. In his book, *Revolutionary Pressures in Africa,* Claude Ake (1977:9) wrote of contradictions that arose between proletarian and bourgeois countries, which has created a class struggle between the two, "brought about revolutionary pressures in Africa" and intensified what he called "mutual alienation." He identified neo-colonial dependency as the most salient feature of a post-colonial African state, a condition that is rooted in, and perpetuated by global class struggle. He concluded that the class war can only be brought to an end through "socialist revolution". This however did not occur, especially with the collapse of the Soviet Union, a country that was passionate about spearheading the global overthrow of the capitalist system. However, there are about half a dozen countries in the continent where revolutionary activities, even if they do not approximate to Claude Ake's prediction, have succeeded. They include, among others, Egypt, Algeria, Ghana, Mozambique, Namibia, and South Africa. Let us briefly examine some of them.

3.6   Egyptian Revolution

The Egyptian Revolution was launched in 1952 by Gamely Abdul Nasser when he led the army to overthrow King Farouk. The revolution began under a revolutionary petty-bourgeois leadership that revolted against the incapacity and corruption of the old regime. It proposed to modernize the country by striking at the old conservative order, and bring about a new era of economic progress that will put to an end the imperialist domination of Egypt. One of the objectives of the revolution was to widen considerably the state sector, a factor that led to the nationalization of heavy industries and big banks including the Suez Canal in 1956. Nasser's administration also granted to the workers and peasant a formal majority of seats in the Egyptian National Assembly. These reforms were meant to actualize the goals of Arab-socialism, which was also anti-capitalist.

Despite these reforms, we must point out that due to a number of reasons Nasser was unable able to create a worker's state. The revolution could not stop free buying and selling of land by the bourgeoisie up to a certain ceiling. Similarly, the state structure inherited from the former regime remained largely intact. There were also no organ of workers power, or independent trade unions, or independent workers' party, and no socialist consciousness among the broad masses. All these have made the private sector to remain very strong, if not dominant. Indeed, apart from the symbolic changes made under Abdul Nasser, the few gains of the revolution were not sustainable, as Nasser successors-Anwar Sadat and Hosni Mubarak- have returned Egypt to the pre-1952 era, especially with their enthusiastic embrace of Western powers, particularly, the United States.

3.7   Ghanaian Revolution

The Ghanaian revolution can be seen from two phases. The first phase was noticed during the struggle for independence by Kwame Nkrumah who advocated for independence for "Self-governance-Now" as

opposed to Dr Joseph Danquah, his counterpart of the United Gold Coast Convention (UGCC), whose slogan was 'Self-Government within the shortest possible time'. What actually made the struggle for independence in Ghana to be regarded as a revolution was that the militancy employed by Nkrumah in his slogans (we prefer self-government in danger to servitude in tranquility) and his eloquent (seek ye first the political freedom and every other thing shall be added unto it), though earned him detention where he won a colonial supervised election, but eventually succeeded in making Ghana the first black African country to gain independence in 1957.

The other phase of the Ghanaian Revolution is the cleansing of the socio-political and economic Augean Stable of Ghana, especially through the execution of three past heads of state Achampong, Afrifa and Akuffo, when Jerry John Rawlings came to power in 1981. He transformed the Ghanaian society by flushing out the corrupt structures and people in the system. Afterwards, he transformed from a military rule to democratic leader, organized a successful transition, and laid the foundation in Ghana of what can now be referred to as an oasis of true democracy in the West African desert of guided or flawed democratic practice.

3.8   Ethiopian Revolution

In the early 1974, Ethiopia entered a period of profound political, economic, and social change, frequently accompanied by violence. One major reason for the Ethiopian revolution was the need to confront the traditional status quo by the modern forces in order to effect meaningful changes in the political, economic and social nature of the Ethiopian state. This is because of the government's failure to effect significant change in the economic and political systems in the country falling standard of living, rising inflation, corruption, and famine which affected several provinces. It is important to note that the 1974 Ethiopian Revolution was initiated by the military, acting essentially in its own immediate interests. But this later spread to the civilian population in an outburst of general dissatisfactions.

Specifically, Colonel Mengistu Haile Mariam led the revolution, which ousted Emperor Haile Salaissi from his authoritarian grip on power and exploitative feudal regime. To some extent, the rule of Mengistu Haile Mariam in Ethiopian is one exemption to the general stereotype of military rule in Africa as an aberration, because his revolution was able to liberate the long-oppressed and exploited working class. It created the necessary conditions for the subsequent rise of the Ethiopian workers Party (EWP), and the Peoples Democratic Republic of Ethiopian

(PDRE), with its own new system of provincial divisions and administration for a socialist government in Ethiopia.

3.9   Algeria, Zimbabwe, Namibia, and South Africa

The revolutions in these Africa countries were struggles to liberate these former colonial territories from an oppressive and exploitative regime of colonial powers. This mostly took the form of guerilla warfare aimed at independence. In Algeria the FLNA led by Ahmed Bembella provided the military vanguard while Frantz Fanon supplied the intellectual sinew; in Zimbabwe Robert Mugabe and Joshua Nkomo of the Patriot Front(an amalgam of ZANU and ZAPU) led the struggle; in Mozambique it was Samoral Machel who piloted the struggle; in Namibia Sam Njuoma was the hero of struggle while, in South Africa, the African National Congress, after it was unbanned and its leader, Nelson Mandela was released from prison in 1990, succeeded in achieving majority rule for the country in 1994.

It is important to note that it was not all liberation struggles in Africa that entailed large scale violence; there were countries such as Nigeria, Sierra Leone and Gambia where independence were negotiated. Equally important is the case of Zimbabwe where Robert Mugabe, after more than three decades in office has succumbed to counter revolutionary forces: manipulation of elections and annihilation of opposition forces to remain in power, economic mismanagement, corruption and gross human rights violations. The only pretences to revolution his regime now show include indiscriminate seizure of white owned farmlands, ostensibly to redress alleged past wrongs, and vitriolic verbal attacks on Western imperialists for interfering in Zimbabwe's internal affairs.

Apart from guerilla wars aimed at independence, African revolution also took internal forms like revolution against despotic and authoritarian leaders. One could cite the example of the overthrow of Mobutu Sese Seko, the sit-tight ruler of former Zaire (now DRC) by Laurent Kabila as another variant of a revolution, since in this case, a corrupt and an unpopular leader was changed in a popular revolt and a new government formed.

SELF-ASSESSMENT EXERCISE 5

Examine the character of revolutionary movements in Africa

4.0   SUMMARY

We have discussed in this unit the concepts of revolution and social change. We identified the conditions that create a revolutionary situation and submitted that a revolution is usually political in character. We also cited examples of revolutionary movements from different countries of the world to illustrate the point that, though the emphasis may differ from one country to the other, the objective of every revolution is to bring about a radical change and institute a new social order.

5.0   CONCLUSION

In view of the conventional bias and bourgeois orientation of political science as a discipline, revolution and social change have become much dreaded terms in the template of political discussion. The reason for this is obvious. The mainstream objective of the major courses in political science is how to promote peace and political stability, a major condition that is needed to ensure economic prosperity. But those who advocate revolution asked the questions: Political stability in whose interest and at what cost? Is stability and peace sustainable without social justice, just like Mahatma Gandhi's proverbial description of the situation in colonial India as "the peace of the grave yard? They therefore argue that not until these pertinent questions are objectively answered can we reasonably conclude whether a call for revolution is justified or not.

6.0   TUTOR-MARKED ASSIGNMENTS

1.   Explain the impacts of 1917 Russian Revolution in inspiring revolutionary situations in other parts of the world.
2.   Discuss the difference between a revolutionary and evolutionary process.
3.   Critically analyze how liberation struggle could assumerevolutionary dimensions.